THE AUDACITY OF GREED

THE AUDACITY OF GREED

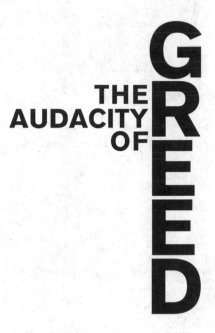

Free Markets, Corporate Thieves, and the Looting of America

Jonathan Tasini

PUBLISHING

Brooklyn, New York

Printed in the United States of America.
10 9 8 7 6 5 4 3 2 1

Ig Publishing
178 Clinton Avenue
Brooklyn, NY 11205
www.igpub.com

Library of Congress Cataloging-in-Publication Data

Tasini, Jonathan.
 The audacity of greed : free markets, corporate thieves and the looting of America / by Jonathan Tasini.
    p. cm.
 ISBN 978-1-935439-00-4
 1. Corporations--Moral and ethical aspects--United States. 2. Ex-ecutives--United States--Conduct of life. 3. Free enterprise--Moral and ethical aspects--United States. 4. Corporate governance--United States. I. Title.
 HF5387.T375 2009
 338.50973--dc22

                                    2009026874

For my father, who would have been disgusted by the greed.

Contents

Introduction: Highway Robbery   9

1. Laying the Groundwork for the Looting of America   20

2. The Club   38

3. The Stock Option Scam   53

4. Vodka and Penises   66

5. The Retirement Jackpot   80

6. How to Screw Up Your Company—And Still Get Rich   93

7. The Wage Cupboard Is Bare   112

8. The Great Collapse   129

9. Conclusion: A Return To Sanity   147

Acknowledgments   172

Notes   173

Introduction: Highway Robbery

The United States of America has just lived through the greatest looting of money in its history, a vast robbery that began in the late 1970s and has stretched to the present day. The perpetrators of this grand robbery didn't just steal a few possessions, or a little bit of cash. Instead, they drained the economy of trillions of dollars, in the process skulking off with a vast fortune that defied imagination while leaving millions of people without jobs, in poverty or without their life savings.

It wasn't a Willie Sutton kind of robbery, with guns drawn and a slip of paper passed to a bank teller. Sutton, you may recall, was a notorious bank robber who lives on in the public imagination because of a one-sentence answer he gave to explain his particular strategy of making money. When asked why he robbed banks, he supposedly replied ("supposedly" because he later denied ever uttering this memorable phrase), "Because that's where the money is." Since Willie was usually well-armed when he committed his crimes, his actions fit well with the classic definition of a robbery, which *Merriam-Webster's Dictionary* tells us is "larceny from the person or presence of another by violence or threat."

No, the robbery I am speaking about was pulled off without a single bullet being fired, and was, for the most part, perfectly legal (though many of the perpetrators actions spilled over into illegality). It was actually more like highway robbery, which *Merriam-Web-*

ster's defines as "excessive profit or advantage derived from a business transaction." You have probably heard of some of the people involved in this highway robbery—Bernard Ebbers, John Rigas, Dennis Kozlowski, Edward Whitacre, Douglas Conant, John Thain, Jeffrey Kindler and David Farr, to name but a few. What do these people all have in common? They are, or were, corporate CEOs.

Over the past few decades, a small group of corporate executives, running mostly American-based companies, have carted off hundreds of billions of dollars—and stand to earn even more riches thanks to incredible pensions. With few exceptions, none of this cadre of executive officers used violence or physical threats (certainly not explicit, documented physical threats) to pull off a systematic looting scheme that is staggering in its scale and breadth across our economy. Instead, with the support of a vast array of accomplices— including academics, media talking heads and politicians across the ideological spectrum, who together helped create the myth of the great CEO, who, as the rap went, had to be paid vast amounts of money because he created so much value for both his company and the economy—pulled off the largest confidence scheme in this country's history.

This great robbery was ideologically enabled by a three decades-long flogging of a worldview that we now know is entirely bankrupt: that our society's well-being is governed by the "free market." The constant rhetorical praise, in newspapers, on TV and by politicians of both parties, of free market ideology—or market fundamentalism—allowed for public acceptance of the robbery, as people were told that the great riches of the CEO were part of the American system of free enterprise, and if they worked hard and played by the rules, they too would one day become wealthy. Ultimately, the free market myth went, we are all part of the big picture of endless American prosperity.

Instead of being based on any kind of sound economic theory, the "free market" was in reality nothing more than a marketing phrase, used to cover up the relentless plundering of our country's prosperity, which was in turn funneled into a small number of hands, creating the deepest divide between rich and poor in more than a century. Look at the numbers; in 2005, the average Chief Executive Officer in the U.S. was paid 821 times as much as a minimum wage earner. Or to put another way—the average CEO earned more before lunchtime on his very first day of work than a minimum wage worker earned during the entire year. And, in a further sign of how audacious the greed of these corporate elites was, at the same time that CEOs were jetting off in their G-5 corporate jets and plunking down $20 million for lavish New York City apartments, workers at their companies were being asked to sacrifice—either by taking a hit in their paychecks, or by being forced to pick up more of their health care costs (or maybe even losing health care all together), all the while looking down the road at the bleak prospects of spending their retirement years without a real pension.

While, on occasion—especially when the excesses or criminal activities of one of the CEOs would be splashed across the headlines—for the most part, the totality of the amount of money these corporate elites took was, until recently, not well understood, nor was the great damage their robbery did to individual companies, the economy as a whole and, most importantly, individual workers. This book tries to capture the overall scale of the robbery, to look at how it was was undertaken and justified, as well as to explain how we can make sure it stops.

Greed is Good...For A Few

I actually began thinking about writing this book before the crash and burn of the financial industry in September 2008, when the world finally discovered that the poster boys for the new Gilded Age, a group of modern day Robber Barons who had pocketed large fortunes, puffing up their egos and their bank accounts largely by piling up huge mountains of debt for their companies, were really little boys with matches who ignited a global economic crisis, obliterating trillions of dollars in wealth in a matter of months.

Let's be clear: greed is the precise reason that millions of people are suffering now and will suffer for years to come. If the CEOs knew one thing, it was how to do their math: the more their company's stock went up or the more cash they could hoard to increase profits, the more their personal fortunes would skyrocket, either because of rich stock options or the personal stakes they held in their companies. Because of greed, many CEOs abandoned basic, sound business practices, building a mountain of debt on pure speculation and inflation of assets. Yes, some wound up losing money, and a few lost great fortunes because of their schemes. But mostly the sky fell in for ordinary people, as millions of jobs were vaporized, with millions more likely to disappear over the next few years; retirement funds, cobbled together over years by people who put off immediate gratification so they could kick back in their golden years, shriveled up.

Like a lot of Americans, I knew the individual stories—the $6,000 shower curtain purchased by Tyco CEO Dennis Kozlowski, the $70 million bonus check for Goldman Sachs' Lloyd Blankfein, the crimes committed by Ken Lay and his cohorts at Enron. But, it wasn't until a Sunday morning in early April 2008 that the enormity of the robbery was really driven home to me. On that day, the business section of *The New York Times* published its annual report on executive pay.[1] There, spread across two full pages, were the salaries, benefits and accumulated wealth of 200 chief executives of large public companies that had filed their proxy statements by the end of the previous month.

As I went down the list, my finger kept stopping at an entry here, an entry there. Total value of equity holdings read one column…$137 million, $122 million, $42 million. The CEO of Occidental Petroluem, Ray Irani, had pulled in $33.6 million in salary and bonuses in 2007 while also adding millions more to his stock option fortune to bring his total equity holdings in the company to $676 million. John Finnegan, the CEO of Chubb, had pocketed almost

$13 million in compensation and boosted his total equity holdings to $42.6 million; his competitor at MetLife, C. Robert Henrickson, had taken home even more in compensation, $14.2 million, with equity holdings of $25 million, all on top of a lump sum retirement pension of $23.3 million (up to that point).

While, at the end of 2007, 46 million Americans had no health care, millions more had inadequate coverage and everyone was paying higher prices for their prescription drugs, pharmaceutical companies such as Merck was paying its CEO Richard Clark $14.4 million; Wyeth was paying its CEO Robert Essner $20 million and Pfizer was giving $12.6 million to its chief executive, Jeffrey Kindler. Pfizer, like their competitors, also made sure that Kindler never sat in his executive suite worrying about his post-employment days, as he had $16.7 million in stock socked away.

By the time I had gotten through scanning the numbers, one thing was apparent—we were talking about a massive fortune that had been collected by a very small number of people. In 2007 alone, the pay and bonuses for those 200 CEOs totaled more than $2.3 billion. In addition, these folks had pocketed lump sum pension benefits totaling almost $1.6 billion and another $1.4 billion in deferred compensation (the pay that they would get after leaving the company, an arrangement that taxpayers are responsible for because there are tax advantages to deferring the compensation). Those 200 CEOs also rang up $1.3 billion in stock option gains and another $646 million in stock award gains. Add all those numbers up and you get a figure of over $4.2 billion in overall wealth. And their pay was just a miniscule portion of the wealth of these CEOs, as at the end of 2007, they held stock valued at $1.4 trillion.

While the 2008 global financial crisis eroded some of that value, tightening the belt in the elite crowd meant foregoing the fourth or fifth mansion, or perhaps hesitating on whether to plunk down millions for a new Matisse or Picasso or waiting one more year to upgrade to a fully-loaded 757 Boeing jet. They were certainly not worrying about making their car payments or paying for health care.

Compared to the guys running the show in the hedge fund and private equity world, however, those 200 CEOs were practically paupers. According to *Institutional Investors Alpha's* annual ranking of the top hedge fund earners, John Paulson, the president of Paulson and Co., ranked number one among his competitors, picking up a cool $3.7 billion in 2007 by betting against a segment of the mortgage industry—meaning that Paulson made a fortune hoping that the housing bubble would burst and millions of people would face foreclosure.[2] To him, though, making money is all about sport and competition, and has nothing to do with human lives: "It's like Wimbledon," Paulson said. "When you win one year you don't quit, you want to win again."[3]

Some of the other large hedge fund earners in 2007 included George Soros, who earned $2.9 billion (which averages out to more than $100,000 per hour) partly by betting against other nation's currencies.[4] It was the same strategy Soros had employed back in the early 1990s, when he made as much as $2 billion speculating against the British pound, giving him the title of "the man who broke the Bank of England."[5] James H. Simons, who runs the hedge fund Renaissance Technologies, made $2.8 billion, while Philip Falcone earned $1.7 billion betting against the mortgage markets, thus making a ton of money hoping that people would lose their homes (though not Falcone personally, as part of his haul paid for the $49 million price tag on a twenty-seven room mansion, decked out with a theater and indoor pool, that he bought from former Penthouse publisher Bob Guccione). And while Kenneth Griffin, President and CEO of Citadel Investment Group, may not have gotten the largest individual paycheck, with an overall net worth of about $3 billion, he sat comfortably in the 117th slot on the list of richest Americans, was married in the garden at Versailles and was able to pay $60 million in 1999 for Cezanne's "Curtain, Jug and Fruit Bowl."

Even more illuminating than the names and numbers on the Institutional Investors Alpha list was how much the wealth of the top hedge fund managers had exploded in just seven years. When the magazine first started its hedge fund rankings in 2002, you needed to make at least $30 million in a given year to be ranked in the top 25. By 2008, however, you would be considered unworthy at that figure, as the privilege of making the top 25 now required you to make at least $360 million. Overall, the top 25 on the 2008 list earned an average of $892 million, an increase of $360 million from the average in 2006.

This greed was also contagious, creating distortions and inefficiencies throughout other industries, including universities, museums, not-for-profit hospitals and foundations. In 2006, the median salary for chief executives at 52 charities that were surveyed by the *Chronicle of Philanthropy* was $288,588, a 7.6 percent increase from 2005. During the same time period, the median base salary of chief executives at large, for profit companies went up just 0.1 percent, meaning that nonprofit executives achieved larger gains in pay as a percentage than executives in the business world.[6]

Among those in the non-profit sector who got in the greed game were Philippe de Montebello, director of the Metropolitan Museum of Art, in New York, who had the highest reported compensation among nonprofit executives at $4,557,342, and Lloyd H. Dean, president of Catholic Healthcare West, who came in second with a compensation of $4,001,892. (Dean's total included a bonus payment of $2,738,656). Third on the list was William R. Brody, president of the Johns Hopkins University, who earned $1,492,220, which included a deferred-compensation benefit of $920,438 that had been accrued in previous years. The top five was rounded out by James J. Mongan, chief executive of Partners HealthCare System, who earned $1,341,650, and Peter Traber, chief executive of Baylor College of Medicine whose take home pay was $1,271,246 in 2006.[7]

The Real World Effects of Corporate Greed

After reading all these extravagant numbers, your reaction may be: so what? A bunch of guys got rich. Big deal. That's the American way. And even if we all agree that these hedge fund managers and CEOs were greedy bastards, in the end, what did it matter? Who did they hurt? While that is certainly a fair question, you have to keep in mind that the personal greed of these corporate elites was but small potatoes in the overall scheme of things. The real reason their greed was so reprehensible was not simply because of what this band of corporate elites managed to hoard for themselves, but the way in which their highway robbery took away the livelihoods and economic security of an entire generation of Americans. It was like Robin Hood in reverse: they took from the poor and working classes, and give to the rich, i.e. themselves.

Focused entirely on their own personal wealth and private aggrandizement, these elites abandoned any loyalty to their workers, their shareholders or their customers and, even though they often cloaked what they did in the patriotic rhetoric of the "free market," to their country. They remained so out of touch with reality that, even at the height of the financial crisis in 2008, they continued to hand each other multi-million dollars bonuses and complained about accepting caps of half-a-million dollars a year (more than the annual salaries of 99 percent of the population) on their compensation in return for getting taxpayer money to bailout their failing institutions. "That is pretty draconian—$500,000 is not a lot of money, particularly if there is no bonus," opined James F. Reda, founder and managing director of James F. Reda & Associates, a compensation consulting firm. As if he hadn't already said enough, Reda continued on, "And you know these companies that are in trouble are not going to pay much of an annual dividend...It would be really tough to get people to staff" companies that are forced to impose these limits...I don't think this will work."[8]

In the end, the affects of CEO greed were felt throughout society. It robbed hard-working people of a decent retirement; it caused hundreds of thousands of people to lose their homes; it meant that nearly 50 million Americans went without health care. CEO greed also meant that millions of people were forced to rack up mountains of debt on their credit cards or leverage the value of their homes to get a new line of credit—not to buy a second home in the South of France or pick up a multi-million yacht, but to pay for health care, college for their kids, care for an aging parent or just to meet their daily bills. CEO greed meant that a whole generation of workers who were duped into substituting their 401(k) plans for real pensions have seen their savings evaporate as a result of plunging stock markets around the world.

CEO greed has also meant that average Americans, if they were not losing their jobs, were being forced into lower paying ones. As Louis Uchitelle wrote in *The New York Times*: "Across America, more than 30 million people have been forced out of jobs since the early 1980s…Nearly 50 million new jobs have been created over that same period…so there are always new opportunities but more often than not at lower pay." Uchitelle added that, "Among those who have lost work, only a third held new jobs two years later that paid as well as those that were lost, according to the bureau's surveys of displaced workers. Another third of those displaced were in jobs that paid, on average, 15 to 20 percent less than their previous employment—while the final third had dropped out of the labor force entirely."[9]

From the Great Depression through the early 1970s, workers were paid, more or less, in proportion to the sweat they poured out on the job. As a result, productivity rose, as did wages. Then, in the 1970s, all that fell apart; productivity went up steadily, but wages stayed flat. As an image, think of the giant open jaw of an alligator, with the top of the jaw, right up to the snout, showing productivity and the bottom of the jaw—representing wages—snapping shut. Not surprisingly, the trail of the benefits of those productivity gains ended right at the bank account of the CEO. While in 1960, CEO pay was 41 times that of the average worker, by 2005, CEO's earned 411 times that of the average worker. And most of that has occurred in the past fifteen years, as the CEO-worker pay gap was "only" 107 to 1 in 1990. Think about it this way: if the minimum wage has risen at the same rate, it would currently be $22.61 per hour.[10]

Stopping the Robbery

Ultimately, the great robbery of the past thirty years has succeeded beyond even the wildest dreams of the corporate elite. According to the *Wall Street Journal*, in 2006, the wealth of the top one percent of Americans "garnered the highest share of the nation's adjusted gross income for two decades, and possibly the highest since 1929, according to Internal Revenue Service data."[11] And did the wealthy at least pay their fair share of taxes, to put something back into a system they had taken so much out of? The same *Wall Street Journal* article reported that the average tax rate of the wealthiest one percent had dropped to its lowest point in almost two decades.[12]

For thirty years, greedy CEOs have ravaged companies, hollowing them out, breaking them up, sucking out their value and leaving them like dry husks—all so that they could enrich themselves beyond anything we have seen in the history of this country. And their actions have been justified to the American people by the concept of the "free market," which says that the top dog can get whatever the market (or his hand-picked board of directors) gives him. Ultimately, the "free market" is the religion that infects our economy, the all-powerful maker of all that is good and all that is prosperous. And the "free market" is also quite a forgiving God, as no matter how often CEOs fail, no matter how many times the people around them, particularly the gurus of finance and corporate-political insiders, turn out to be wrong and screw up the economy, they continue to reign—over their companies, or as advisors to presidents and national political leaders, or as figures sought after by the media seeking wise advice and perspective.

To fix all this, we can't just call for more regulation. Instead, we need a cultural and philosophical revolution that punctures the fable of the great CEO, stops the robbery and, by doing so, values the contributions made by workers throughout the economy. Have we done so? The answer, as we will see at the end of this book, is sadly no. Can we change this? The answer is emphatically yes.

In thinking about our future as a nation, I am reminded of the moving criticism made by Pastor Martin Niemöller of the German intellectuals who ignored the Nazi rise to power in the 1930s: "In Germany they first came for the Communists, and I didn't speak up because I wasn't a Communist. Then they came for the Jews, and I didn't speak up because I wasn't a Jew. Then they came for the trade unionists, and I didn't speak up because I wasn't a trade unionist. Then they came for the Catholics, and I didn't speak up because I was a Protestant. Then they came for me —and by that time no one was left to speak up."

There has been a great moral crime committed upon millions of Americans. Until now, too many people have stood by, refusing to speak up because they thought that as long as it didn't hit them personally, the immorality could be ignored. As we have certainly learned over the past year, it cannot be ignored any longer.

1. Laying the Groundwork for the Looting of America

The great robbery this country has lived through for the past three decades wouldn't have been as successful as it has been without a long-term, persistent barrage of ideas that has been rained down upon the American people, a deluge that was—and still is—promoted and celebrated each and every day, seeping into our brains via a relentless, non-stop mantra advanced by every traditional media outlet, whether "liberal" or "conservative," and via the rhetoric—and actions—of most politicians, Republican or Democrat.

It's similar to a con game played by hustlers in New York City's Times Square. A quick-talking man will show you a pea, put the pea under one of three cups, quickly shuffle the cups around and then ask you to point to the cup under which you think the pea now rests. Most times, of course, you point to the wrong cup; you think you've kept track of the pea but then it's gone—along with your money.

Instead of three cups and a pea, the people behind the looting of America have used a whole host of constantly evolving phrases and terms—competiveness, free enterprise, free trade, a global economy, to name but a few—to sell their ideas to the public, screaming and jumping up and down as they yelled at us through the TV screen, antics necessary to distract us from the deeds that were going on behind the scenes. They told us we were getting poorer because of government bureaucrats who wasted our money, when in reality it was an unfair tax system that was robbing the government of its ability to serve us. They wanted us to believe, at a time when corporate profits were soaring to record levels and CEOs were earning tens of millions of dollars, that companies couldn't afford to provide good-paying jobs to their workers. They told us that if we wanted to have a secure retirement, we shouldn't wait for Social Security or expect our employers to give us a decent pension, but that instead we should have faith in the stock market. And they said that we shouldn't blame the private health insurance industry, which was raking in large profits at the expense of people's lives, for the disastrous health care system; instead, blame the poor and elderly who use Medicare and Medicaid when they get sick.

Behind all this shouting and misdirection was a singular ideology: Market Fundamentalism. To the pundits on television, the politicians in government and the executives running America's largest companies, Market Fundamentalism was—and still is, despite the economic calamity of the past year—the great decider on all questions about the economy. Thus, everything has to be considered within the framework of the market. For example: Want to curb CEO greed? Nope—market fundamentalism dictates that a single person can crown himself the most important individual in a company, worthy of a king's ransom, while his "subjects"—the hundreds or thousands of workers who make the company run—get pennies.

My favorite definition of the term comes from the Longview Institute, a think tank started by several of the founders of the Rockridge Institute (famous for the work of George Lakoff). Longview defines market fundamentalism as "the exaggerated faith that when markets are left to operate on their own, they can solve all economic and social problems." Market fundamentalism has dominated the public policy debate in the United States since the 1980s, in the process "serving to justify huge Federal tax cuts, dramatic reductions in government regulatory activity, and continued efforts to downsize the government's civilian programs." While Republicans and conservatives have long been the chief proponents of the tenets of market fundamentalism, "many Democrats and liberals have also accepted much of this mistaken belief system."[1]

According to Longview, there are seven market fundamentalist "myths" which this country's economic policy has, for the past quarter century, been based upon:

1. The market is the only source of innovation and it must be left alone if we want to accelerate technological change.
2. Government will always spend money less productively than private citizens; this is why tax cuts are almost always a good idea.
3. Regulation of business is wasteful, unproductive and usually unnecessary.
4. Financial markets thrive when regulation is kept to a minimum.
5. Private firms will always produce a good or a service more efficiently than the government.
6. It is wrong to regulate wages or executive compensation because markets always get prices right.
7. Government assistance always ends up hurting the people it is supposed to help.[2]

The big daddy of market fundamentalism is the phrase "Free Market." When the words "free market" are uttered by a politician or a pundit, it is meant to be hypnotic, designed to stop any counterview. If you are thinking about pushing for a tax increase on the wealthiest Americans or arguing for a role for government in regulating business or trying to halt bad trade deals, hearing the term "free market" is supposed to make you snap to, as if you are a sleeper agent being given a code that awakens you to a new reality, a reality in which you are now part of the "free market" team. And the "free market" team was—at least until 2008—offering you quite a deal: let the market operate on its own—"free"—and all of us will be the recipients of endless prosperity. In short, the American Dream.

Those who believe in the myths of market fundamentalism do

so with a religious fundamentalist fervor, because, like fundamentalists in Christianity, Judaism, or Islam, their faith is blind, intolerant of opposing views and, most importantly, cannot be proven. You just have to believe in market fundamentalism, no questions asked. Therefore, as long as you declare your faith in the "free market," you are an acceptable politician, no matter your ideological affiliation. For example, every president—regardless of party identification—since Ronald Reagan (and indeed, since Jimmy Carter, as we shall see) has embraced the concept of the free market. "We know how to secure a more just and prosperous life for man on Earth: through free markets, free speech, free elections, and the exercise of free will unhampered by the state," declared George H.W. Bush in his 1989 inauguration speech. His successor in the White House, Bill Clinton proved his allegiance to the "free market" by signing the North American Free Trade Agreement, commonly known as NAFTA. (Clinton's wife, former Senator and current Secretary of State Hillary Clinton, has long shared her husband's free trade philosophy, declaring in a 1997 speech to the Corporate Council on Africa that, "The simple fact is, nations with free-market systems do better."[3])

Even in the midst of an historic economic collapse, then President Bush could still brazenly stick to the "free market" script. "The crisis was not a failure of the free-market system, and the answer is not to try to reinvent that system," Bush said in a November 2008 speech at Federal Hall in downtown Manhattan. "Free-market capitalism is far more than an economic theory. It is the engine of social mobility, the highway to the American dream."[4] And while many believe that the recent government stimulus because of the economic meltdown shows that President Obama is not a true market fundamentalist like his predecessors, the fact remains that Obama's economic inner circle is made up of free market ideologues like Lawrence Summers and Timothy Geithner, both of whom are disciples of the original free market peddler, Robert Rubin.

"We will be a long-term winner in this industry"

How did this blind of allegiance to the "free market" begin? And why has it been so successful? Before we start, you need to keep in mind this fact: market fundamentalism is a failure, if you define the success of any economic theory in a modern society as a set of ideas that is supposed to bring about broad-based prosperity. In fact, until the 1970s, market fundamentalism was a fringe, not very well-thought of theory because, generally speaking, most of the political and economic leaders around the world understood that a strong mix of public—meaning government—and private interaction was a good thing.

Starting in the 1970s, however, a number of things happened to push market fundamentalism into the forefront of economic theory. First off, great sums of money began to pour into a network of institutes, think tanks and university-based projects. Bankrolled by millions of dollars, the goal of these largely conservative groups was to position market fundamentalism as the undisputed foundation of the American economic engine. While these groups got the ball rolling, I would mark the rise of Paul Volker (another Obama advisor) as head of the Federal Reserve Board as the opening salvo in the three-decade long market fundamentalism attack.

For many years, the United States had an economic policy based on full employment, balanced with the idea of price stability. But, in 1979, all that changed with a Volker-led change in monetary policy. As David Harvey writes in his book *A Brief History of Neoliberalism*: "The long-standing commitment in the US liberal democratic state to the principles of the New Deal, which meant broadly Keynesian fiscal and monetary policies with full employment as the key objective, was abandoned in favor of a policy designed to quell inflation no matter what the consequences might be for employment."[5] Therefore, it no longer mattered how many people were out of work as long as prices did not rise so much that financiers became upset about the value of their investments.

Volker's policy fit hand-in-glove with the bipartisan rush to deregulation that started with Jimmy Carter and which was grabbed enthusiastically by his successor, Ronald Reagan. Thus, the idea that nothing should stand in the way of the wisdom of the market took hold among the political, economic and media ruling classes, affecting every area of commerce. For example—manage prices by regulating airline fares? That went out the door in the 1970s in favor of cutthroat competition (enjoy flying these days?). Oversee the savings-and-loan industry with tight regulation? That type of control went out the window at a cost of half-a-billion dollars, which was the price tag for the decade-long cleanup from 1986 to 1995 of the wreckage of more than 1,000 failed S&L's (the cost of that debacle was actually much higher since troubles in the industry began earlier than the figures compiled once the government stepped in).[6]

By the dawn of the twenty-first century, the "free market" had become the unquestioned economic rule of the land, adopted by those across the political spectrum. While it would not surprise anyone to read lengthy quotes from deeply conservative thinkers like William F. Buckley extolling the virtues of the "free market," you could also find Robert F. Kennedy, Jr., an ardent environmentalist and liberal, declaring: "I want to say this: There is no stronger advocate for free market capitalism than myself. I believe that the free market is the most efficient and democratic way to distribute the goods of the land, and that the best thing that could happen to the environment is if we had true free market capitalism in this country, because the free market promotes efficiency, and efficiency means the elimination of waste, and pollution of course is waste. The free market also would encourage us to properly value our natural resources, and it's the undervaluation of those resources that causes us to use them wastefully."[7]

Flash forward to today, and the concept of protecting the "free market" has become so ingrained in the American psyche that, even at the height of the economic crisis in 2009, President Obama sought to tamp down on the waves of public rage that were cascading across the nation against the financial bailout of banks and Wall

Street firms by saying that "in a time of crisis, we cannot afford to govern out of anger, or yield to the politics of the moment."[8] At the same time, however, we were told that the "free market" could not tolerate government intervention to save bankrupt auto companies (and the jobs of unionized auto workers) or exercise control over the nation's banking system, as such measures could be considered "European-like."[9]

Unfortunately, our long-term obedience to the ideology of market fundamentalism has meant that we have entrusted our financial security to a cadre of economists, investors, business people and politicians who have utterly mismanaged our economy, failing in the most basic mission entrusted to them: to provide a real, shared prosperity for *all* citizens. And yet, despite the overwhelming evidence that they simply couldn't be trusted, the people who got us into our current economic mess are still asked to serve in our government and are still sought after for advice. While I am certainly making an ideological argument here, I also think the hard economic facts speak for themselves. Over the past thirty years, we have had more than one asset bubble popping or calamity that struck the country (and the world) that was attributable to the people who preached the wonders of the "free market." There was the savings and loan crisis of the 1980s, the internet bubble of the 1990s, and, most recently, the housing bubble. In each case, while hard working "regular" people suffered, the "free market" cheerleaders kept on scamming the system.

Take Citigroup, as one example among many. Looking back to November 2008, the company had posted four consecutive quarters of losses, and had written off billions of dollars. According to *The New York Times*, "nine of its investment funds have cratered this year. And now the bank could face a tsunami of new losses in its once-lucrative consumer loan business as the global economy weakens."[10] In addition to its own economic woes, the bank had also played a central role in the country's economic collapse by underwriting the subprime mortgage and credit-default swap markets. Despite these catastrophic failures, Citigroups's CEO Vikram Pandit declared in late 2008 that the company was "entering 2009 in a strong position, much stronger than we entered in 2008…We will be a long-term winner in this industry."[11]

Strong position? The company had just announced it would lay-off 52,000 workers. And there you have it in a nutshell: Citigroup had helped make a mess of itself and the economy, but dumping tens of thousands of workers was seen as the right "free market" move to make the company strong again. And, despite multiple "free market" failures, "leaders" such as Pandit are still paid outrageous sums—to the tune of $38 million for Pandit in 2008[12]—as long as they stick with the "free market" faith…a faith that seemed a bit, shall we say, misplaced for Citigroup, since it received $45 billion in taxpayer bailout money from the government in 2008.[13]

"Disturbingly Protectionist"

One of the main offshoots of the "free market" is "free trade," i.e. when goods and services are "bought and sold between countries or sub-national regions without tariffs, quotas or other restrictions being applied."[14] The concept of free trade is based largely upon the theory of comparative advantage, which is defined by the Bureau for Labor Statistics as "When one nation's opportunity cost of producing an item is less than another nation's opportunity cost of producing that item. A good or service with which a nation has the largest absolute advantage (or smallest absolute disadvantage) is the item for which they have a comparative advantage."[15]

In particular since the passage of NAFTA in the early 1990s, "free trade" has been an integral component of the market fundamentalist push toward a so-called global economy. In this worldview, when trade barriers such as tariffs come down, opportunity will increase for workers throughout the world, raising everyone's standard of living.

Those who believe, on the other hand, that "free trade" is damaging to workers and destructive to the environment have long been labeled as "protectionists" by the market fundamentalists. As the economist Robert Kuttner writes, "Ever since the economist David Ricardo offered the basic theory in 1817, economic scripture has taught that open trade, free of tariffs, quotas, subsidies, or other government distortions, improves the well-being of both parties. US policy has implemented this doctrine with a vengeance, and opponents are seen as self-serving losers."[16] As an example of this anti-protectionist rhetoric, a 1993 *Wall Street Journal* article on NAFTA declared that "if protectionism spreads, unchecked by a strong, persistent free-trade champion, the growth of international trade could slow down in coming decades. And the world's economies would pay a heavy price."[17] Similarly, in the famous 1993 debate between then vice president Al Gore and Ross Perot on NAFTA, Gore tried to blame protectionism for the Great Depression, saying, in reference to the Smoot-Hawley Tariff Act of 1930, "They raised tariffs, and it was one of the principal causes—many economists say the principal cause—of the Great Depression in this country and around the world."[18] Time hasn't altered the rhetoric much, as during the 2008 presidential race, an editorial in the *Financial Times* criticized then candidate Obama's anti-NAFTA rhetoric as "disturbingly protectionist."[19]

Once he became the nominee, however, Obama's "protectionist" rhetoric seemed to magically disappear, as by June 2008 he had backed off his pledge to unilaterally reopen negotiations on NAFTA.[20] By June of 2009, just one year later, President Obama had fully adopted both the ideology and rhetoric of "free trade"; in speaking on a provision in the Waxman-Markley energy bill that would impose trade penalties on countries that did not accept limits on global warming pollution, Obama warned that, "'At a time when the economy worldwide is still deep in recession and we've seen a significant drop in global trade, I think we have to be very careful about sending any protectionist signals out there.'"[21]

NAFTA was the first salvo in the market fundamentalists push toward a global economy based on free trade. Negotiated by Republican George H.W. Bush and passed by Democrat Bill Clinton, the agreement went into effect in 1994 with the promise that the then small U.S. trade deficit with Mexico and Canada would turn into a surplus as the United States became an export engine for manufactured goods. Gary Hufbauer and Jeffrey Schott of the International Institute of Economics, both major supporters of NAFTA, wrote that the agreement would create "about 170,000 net new US jobs" by 1995,[22] and would "maintain an annual current account surplus with Mexico of about $10 billion throughout the 1990s."[23]

The reality? The Economic Policy Institute estimated that NAFTA had cost the United States approximately one million jobs as of 2006, many of them good-paying manufacturing jobs that were the backbone of America's middle class.[24] As far as the trade surplus, since NAFTA was enacted, the United States has accumulated more than $1.2 trillion in trade *deficits* to both Mexico and Canada.[25] In addition, wages in Canada now lag behind U.S. wages, and the average Mexican wage has also plummeted. Beyond the statistics, the effect of NAFTA on this country has been devastating, as workers haunted by the specter of losing their jobs have become more fearful of forming unions or striking—and companies have used that fear to break union organizing drives and drive down wages and benefits.

What went wrong? Actually, nothing—NAFTA worked perfectly, if one understands that it was an agreement designed to make life easier for corporations, not regular workers. Blinded by the tens of millions of dollars spent by corporate interests to push the treaty and the backroom deals made by Bill Clinton to buy votes for its passage, Congress either did not see, or did not want to admit, that companies were not as interested in exporting goods as they were in exporting jobs.

The core problem is that so-called "free trade" treaties have, in fact, little to do with trade; that is, the reduction of tariffs and elimination of quotas. In reality, these agreements have created a set of economic rules whose primary purpose is to protect capital and investment, including the expansion of monopoly patent rights on drugs and other goods; the extension of intellectual property rights (for corporations, not individual authors and artists); the privatization and deregulation of services; and the weakening or "harmonization" (dropping higher standards to be in sync with lower standards) of food safety standards. "Free trade" agreements have also allowed companies to attack prevailing wage laws and create agricultural policies that have displaced millions of peasant farmers, increasing hunger, social unrest and desperate worker migration throughout the world.

Whenever lawmakers have expressed concerns about the possible negative effects these agreements have on workers and the environment, the free trade cheerleaders have blunted their criticism by including provisions in the treaties that supposedly enforce labor and environmental standards, but in reality do neither. For example, during the debate over NAFTA, several members of Congress worried that "the extreme differences between U.S. and Mexican wages, labor laws, and levels of economic development would result in significant U.S. job loss."[26] To placate these critics, the Clinton Administration negotiated the North American Agreement on Labor Cooperation to "promote compliance with, and effective enforcement by each Party of, its labor law." The NAALC created the Commission for Labor Cooperation, which was supposed to ensure the agreement's implementation. The budget of the CLC was to be funded by all three NAFTA signees, with the U.S government providing a $2 million-a year appropriation. But, as Public Citizen, the nonprofit consumer advocacy organization, discovered, "In another example of the gap between promised authorizations and actual funds appropriated to such programs, the CLC has only been granted $7.2 million of the $22 million it was authorized to receive from the United States as of 2005, or less than a third of the promised amount."[27] Unfortunately, this was not an isolated case; after reviewing "all 93 trade vote deals we could unearth starting in 1992 with NAFTA," Public Citizen found that "only 11 percent of the policy deals were kept…a bipartisan standard of betrayal covering the first and [then] current Bush administrations and two Clinton terms."[28]

In the end, it appears that the "protectionists" were, based on the evidence, correct on the merits of free trade. As economists Dean Baker and Mark Weisbrot wrote in 2007, "The U.S. economy during a period in which it was mostly a closed economy (1946 to 1973) vastly outperformed the increasingly open economy that we have had over the last 33 years, in terms of raising living standards."[29] The key point here is that workers in this country did better in the "closed economy" than under an economy that promotes "free trade."

As far as the effect of "free trade" on the rest of the world, according to Weisbrot, "If we ignore income distribution and just look at income per person—the most basic measure of economic progress that economists use—the last quarter-century has been a disaster." During the period from 1960 to 1980, adjusting for inflation, per capita income in Latin America grew by 82 percent. However, over the next twenty years, it grew by only 9 percent; and only four percent from 2000 to 2005. To find a stagnant growth period in Latin America that is even close to that, "one has to go back more than a century, and choose a 25-year period that includes both World War I and the start of the Great Depression."[30]

A Glass is Just A Glass

A corollary of the "free trade" hustle is the supposed need for workers to get educated in order to compete in the new, global marketplace. Since the passage of NAFTA, the people of this country have heard repeatedly that the solution to inadequate wages, disappearing heath care, vanishing pensions and staggering personal debt is greater education for workers. Hardly a day goes by when politicians or pundits don't slip in a plug for a "smarter" workforce. While this may sound correct on the surface—after all, who is against education?—it is in fact an utterly disingenuous response to the question of how to cope with the effect the current model of "free trade" is having on the American workforce.

The education rap has been embraced by both liberals and conservatives. Chief among the "education is salvation" advocates on the left is former Clinton Labor Secretary Robert Reich. There was a time in the 1990s when it seemed as if Reich was everywhere, promoting his "Field of Dreams" theory of job creation. According to Reich, if workers would just get educated and retrained, they would have nothing to fear, particularly of so-called "free trade," because the future of the nation lay in "symbolic analysts." This was not, as we had been told, about the fear of moving into the future. It was not about whether the glass was half-full or half-empty. It was actually the problem of the glass itself.

In August 1994, Reich was laying out his "Field of Dreams" theory before an audience convened by the Center for National Policy at the Hyatt Regency in Washington, D.C. Standing at the lectern, he was reading more or less from a prepared text when he decided suddenly to stray. Picking up a drinking glass sitting at his elbow, he said:

> Take this glass next to me and you see that what you are paying for, what a consumer is actually paying for is less and less related to the actual production that goes into making the glass, more and more into the design engineering, the marketing, the legal services, all of the management consulting services, the distribution services, all of the services that go into making up this glass. These are not necessarily bad jobs, some of them are very good jobs, some of them are highly skilled jobs. We've got to make sure that more and more Americans get those kind of jobs.[31]

While Reich's theory of the glass sounded convincing to those seated in the audience, in fact, his entire theory was demonstrably wrong or, at best, he conveniently told only one side of the story. I decided to track the glass Reich had held in his hand and found out that, at the time, its wholesale cost was ninety-five cents and that it was called an Arctic Pattern, made by J.G. Durand, a privately-held French company with more than 12,000 employees worldwide. Although about 800 people worked for the company in the U.S. at the time, the "Arctic Pattern [is] mostly produced in France," a company spokesperson told me. More importantly, she said there was almost *zero* design engineering value in this glass—because it had been around, in 1994, for twenty years.

In addition, Libby, Inc., a unionized Durand competitor at the time, made a very similar glass called the Winchester. Wayne Zitkus, the company's technical manager, completely contradicted Reich's theory that production costs were declining. "I don't think that's generally true" he told me. In fact, he said, "labor costs are very high, energy and materials, those costs have all increased over the years" and accounted for more of the company's production costs. He added that the basic design of his company's glass had been done ten years before.

Even more revealing, Zitkus said that although the industry had entered into a higher-automated computer age, his company still didn't require people with higher levels of education for most of its jobs—the central contention of Reich's "Field of Dreams" theory. With the exception of a few advanced jobs, did most workers need more skills, I asked? "Probably not," Zitkus said. "We're probably measuring people the same way [we did] ten years ago. We have tests to give to people to see whether they have general mechanical skills that we need. We're educating people ourselves. We've trained people so rather than turn knobs they're looking at numbers." The most important fact from this whole episode was that what computer automation had done was not raise the required skills level of workers, but instead had eliminated 35,000 jobs in the glass-making industry in a decade. And nobody had been able to find any direct connection between technological progress and skill upgrading—as Zitkus himself illustrated.

Reich's "Field of Dreams" job theory was a way for him to play both sides of the coin—supporting "free trade," which would be devastating to millions of workers, but, at the same time, showing concern for their future by exhorting them to just get smarter (read: educated). In truth, it is declining wages, not skills or education that are the most important issue facing workers today. The disparity in wages is so great that American workers, no matter how smart or educated they become, will never be able to compete against workers in other countries—unless, of course, Americans are willing to accept a drastic decline in their standard of living.

Though I've written repeatedly over the years about education as a phony solution to the depressed wages of American workers, I also understand its allure, as it is an easy solution for most people to grasp. It also plays into the view that, if we simply better educate the American workforce, then this country will "win" out in the economic global competition because ultimately we're smarter and better than "the others." Most Americans still think of China and India and other "Third World" countries as places where massive plants turn out lower-skilled products (assembly-line electronics, clothes and other durable goods). Reflecting this view, in 2007, *New York Times* columnist Thomas Friedman asked, "What can many U.S. companies still manufacture?" His answer? "They can manufacture things that are smart—that have a lot of knowledge content in them, like a congestion pricing network for a whole city. What do many Chinese companies manufacture? They manufacture things that can be made with a lot of cheap labor, like the rubber tires on your car. Which jobs are most easily outsourced? The ones vulnerable to cheap labor. Which jobs are hardest to outsource? Those that require a lot of knowledge."[32] Like Friedman (and Reich), many Americans are content to let countries like China and India do all the "cheap" work, while we supposedly corner the market on higher-end stuff like airplanes and biotechnology products (and congestion pricing networks). In reality, though, China is well on its way to making products up and down the skill level—at a fraction of the labor cost. In his book *The Chinese Century*, Oded Shenkar writes that, "China's goal, and that of its government is not merely to catch up with the major industrialized powers but to overpass them. No other developing country has sets its sights so high, and none...has laid such a detailed road map to take it there."[33] Friedman and Reich are purveyors of the view—repeated by most Republicans, too many Democrats, as well as numerous academics and political analysts—that education is the salvation for workers trying to survive in the new global economy. But, the truth is that view is a cruel hoax. Friedman has it partly right when he talks about cheap labor—but that cheap labor extends up and down the ladder at all levels of manufacturing. Yes, China is making your clothes—but it is also designing jet engines, and investing heavily in bio-technology and computer research, to mention just a few areas. The reality is that the competition in the world is simply about who will do the work cheapest—whether you are sewing on buttons or coming up with the newest "green" technology.

Ultimately, focusing on the false choice of worker "education" is a whole lot easier than trying to put an end to "free trade," which would entail imposing some community investment demands on the flow of capital and demanding worldwide minimum standards that stop the ferocious competition based solely on who pays the lowest wages. In our current economic circumstances, an "educated workforce" cannot be the sole answer to the challenge of global competition. Until we are willing to confront the effect of corporate power on "free trade," workers may hang diplomas on their walls, but they won't be able to feed their families.

Value Workers...Devalue CEOs

The power of the "free market" lie has also created another troubling phenomenon: politicians and pundits who blame *employees* for the troubles of American companies, and believe that the solution to the economic problems of corporations is for workers to give up a portion of their wages, pensions and health care.

During the latter half of 2008, we lived through the daily spectacle of auto workers being thrashed in the traditional media. During that time, I was involved in a number of television debates with a variety of pundits who were quick to blame workers for the troubles of the auto industry. The rap was always the same: the autoworkers should make deep concessions to save the industry because at the core of the problem were autoworkers' "gold-plated" benefits and "generous" pensions.

This kind of argument underscores the iron grip that the "free market" refrain has on our DNA. In fact, the economic crisis we have descended into over the past year is not the fault of workers or the unions they belong to, but is a consequence of the unbridled greed and incompetence of a handful of corporate executives and a concurrent blind belief in a failed economic model that tells workers, in the name of "competitiveness" and "free trade," that they have to accept lower wages and fewer benefits. For example, workers have been told over the past decade that real pensions—a check they could count on each and every month—were a thing of the past, and that the glory of the "free market" would make their 401(k) plans burst at the seams. But, like the rest of the "free market" mantra, the 401(k) hustle was just a clever way of blowing up the promise of an American community and replacing it with a world where each individual has to fight to get his or her piece of an ever shrinking pie while an elite class siphons money away from the average worker.

Despite what free market ideology might tell us, the problems in our economy are not the fault of the autoworker, the firefighter, the teacher or the secretary. They are not the ones who made poor management decisions; they aren't the ones who looted their companies. When we hear the story of the "overpaid" union member, we have to be courageous enough to understand that these are nothing more than the lies and misrepresentations of people who have never worked in an auto plant, never crawled through dangerous subway tunnels, never had to carry sixty pounds of equipment into a burning building and never had to slaughter animals at numb-minding speeds.

While specific policies such as single-payer health insurance, a more progressive tax structure, increased unionization and a new trade policy that is not based on the search for the lowest wage possible would certainly change the economic structure of this country, what we really need is a new culture which values contributions from workers over the "expertise" of the CEO. In our current audacity of greed, the elite corporate class has come to value themselves so highly that they feel entitled—by the "free market"—to take a gargantuan share of the wealth in this country, leaving crumbs for the rest of us. In essence, they are saying that their contributions matter far more than that of ordinary workers. But from where I sit, I notice the CEO far less than I do the sanitation worker, the firefighter, the teacher, and the whole gamut of people who make this country run. What we need is a reinvigorated valuation of the contributions of the working class in this country, as well as a stem-to-stern rewriting of the rules that structure how our economy works, so that we can replace phony—and dangerous—marketing phrases like "free market" and "free trade" with a system that represents a more equitable, democratic economy.

2. The Club

Anyone who commits a robbery—particularly on a grand scale—needs accomplices. You just can't pull off a big-time heist—especially one stretching over months, and in several instances, years—without assistance. The CEO Robber Barons were no different, as they got help at every level of the game.

Theirs was a complex scheme, which used intricate rules, legal bribes (often called "campaign contributions") and a lot of rhetoric about the "free market" to act both as a cover and to give their heist intellectual legitimacy. The CEO Robber Barons needed for everyone involved in the financial system—from corporate board members to government regulators to politicians—to look the other way in order to undercut any serious efforts at governance or reform. These accomplices were members of what I call "The Club."

Members of The Club all had different roles in the looting of America, and were rewarded in various ways depending on their role. Getting into The Club usually meant you could pocket a nice salary for doing very little work—such as agreeing to serve on a company's board of directors—or, if you were a politician, receive help to remain in office thanks to the cash the CEO Robber Barons aimed your way come election time.

The job of The Club was perhaps most important in creating a justification for the greed of the corporate elite. For example, the most common argument for paying outlandish salaries to CEOs has long been that "the market" dictates the necessity of such a high level of pay. However, who and what exactly is "the market"? It isn't some mythical, amorphous God, dispassionate and all-knowing, possessing other-worldly powers and insight, which hands down the rules of competition that snags these special human beings. No, the market is, in fact, the members of The Club. En masse, they descended on television talk shows, lobbied Congress, met each other at private parties and dispensed their wisdom to compensation consultants. It was—and is—a self-perpetuating, self-reinforcing echo chamber; the CEOs would regurgitate the nonsense about needing to keep pay competitive, and then hire a small circle of compensation consultants, who themselves earned huge fees to make sure that CEO pay went up. Since they all traveled in the same circles, the members of The Club would repeat, like robots, the "free market" argument about CEO pay—which was, in turn, picked up by executives and reporters in the mainstream media, all of whom were either part of The Club or, in the case of journalists, people who wanted to continue to have access to the CEOs and other members of The Club. This incestuous circle occurred across the media and political spectrum, regardless of ideology.

And The Club was not simply an American phenomenon. Indeed, the looting of this country could not have happened without The Club having gone global. Think of the chain this way: a CEO would look for a way to increase revenues for his company; if he could do it by chopping wages or benefits or laying off people, all the better. But, in many cases, it was easier to lower costs and save money by shifting jobs overseas, exploiting cheap labor in China and other countries.

All this was enabled by the world of so-called "free trade," whose cop on the beat is the World Trade Organization. The WTO, as one of its staff members put it, "is the place where governments collude in private against their domestic pressure groups."[1] When it comes to trade, the U.S. government—and, frankly, the majority of governments around the world—are represented by professional lawyers (many of whom come from corporate lobbying backgrounds) who are devoted to the mission of advancing the "free trade" mission. As consumer advocate Ralph Nader puts it, "The first thing a dictator wants is for no one to know what he's doing...The whole W.T.O. process is a marvelous collage of privileged exclusion to make decisions while groups of the citizenry don't know what's going on and aren't free to participate in these power plays."[2]

For the members of The Club, "free trade" was, and is, a very useful and powerful weapon, as it gives off the impression that the elite is working on behalf of the citizenry—even if, at the end of the day, broad prosperity did not arise from "free trade," except if you were a member of The Club, who usually profited quite handsomely.

Robert Rubin—President of the Club

In order to sustain the looting of corporate treasuries and the public domain without drawing too much attention to what you are doing, you need to have someone to justify your actions, someone who is able to traverse the worlds of finance, politics and media, a person who evinces a sense of calm, and who, just by virtue of his reputation, can put everyone's minds at ease. No one has been more adept at filling that role than Robert Rubin, the classic example of the fixer who moves easily between the political and economic elites, smoothing the path for the "free market."

A quick perusal of Rubin's professional life reads like the tale of a paragon of privilege, mixing service in the corporate world with do-gooder roles that convey an aura of social and cultural engagement. On one hand, he had a three-decade career at Goldman Sachs, where he rose quickly from an associate position in 1966 to a general partner in 1971, becoming a member of the company's management committee in 1980 and, finally, vice chairman and co-chief operating officer from 1987 to 1990. Consistent with his elite leadership status, Rubin was also a member of the Board of Directors of the New York Stock Exchange, the Harvard Management Company, the New York Futures Exchange, the President's Advisory Committee for Trade Negotiations and the Securities and Exchange Commission Market Oversight—all positions where he was able to dispense his market wisdom and help shape economic policy. On the other hand, his resume is also peppered with a whole raft of "selfless" service, including sitting on the Board of Trustees of Mount Sinai-NYU Health and the Carnegie Corporation of New York—all done presumably to help open the political and non-profit fundraising doors to the Wall Street and financial worlds.

Casting aside the resume lines, let us zero in on Rubin's biggest role in the economy: for the better part of two decades, he has been the person most active in uniting the political elite with the economic interests of Wall Street, pushing The Club's agenda items of using increased debt and leverage to boost profits and reduce government regulation, as well as flogging the idea that the nation had to practice "fiscal responsibility" and get rid of those big, bad deficits.

When Bill Clinton entered the White House in 1993, he tapped Rubin to be the first director of the National Economic Council. Rubin was, in many ways, the point person on pushing NAFTA and expanding the so-called "free trade" agenda, which was, as I pointed out in chapter one, simply about expanding the opportunities for United States based firms to pour investment and capital into developed and emerging economies without being hindered by troublesome restraints such as country-specific rules about protecting agriculture, labor or the environment. Of course, as a full-fledged member of The Club, Rubin was always looking out for his sidekicks. Robert Kuttner astutely observed that, "After NAFTA created a gold rush of foreign money pouring into Mexico, enriching Goldman Sachs and its clients and triggering an unsustainable speculative boom followed by a crash, Rubin promoted the bailout of Mexico that made foreign bondholders whole. A little-noticed provision of NAFTA permitted foreign banks to acquire Mexican ones. In 2001, Rubin, back in the private sector, negotiated Citigroup's $12.5 billion acquisition of Mexico's leading bank, Banamex."[3]

Rubin also was front and center in the drive to tear down the wall between commercial and investment banks—a wall that had existed since the 1933 Glass-Steagall Act and had been erected precisely to prevent the kind of speculation that had ripped through the heart of the economy in the 1920s, triggering the collapse of the stock market and ushering in the Great Depression. You had two powerful ideas banging up against each other here. On the one side, keeping the highly regulated commercial lending banks separate from the mostly unregulated investment banks meant that regulators—and, in theory, Congress—could keep track of how financial assets were moving through the system to prevent any unscrupulous or destabilizing shenanigans from taking place. On the other side, you had investment bankers who pined after the profits that could be made—through fees and deals—if the wall came down.

Guess who won?

To get the answer, ask Brooksley Born. Born was about as establishment as you could get: a graduate of Stanford Law School and a partner, until she retired, in Arnold & Porter, one of Washington D.C.'s premier lobbying and legal powerhouses. From 1996 to 1999, she served as the chair of the Commodity Futures Trading Commission, the federal agency that regulates options and futures trading. In 1997, Born told Congress that the trading of derivatives without any kind of regulation could "threaten our regulated markets or, indeed, our economy without any federal agency knowing about it." She also told Congress something that a decade later would show her to be quite prescient: "Losses resulting from misuse of OTC derivatives instruments or from sales practice abuses in the OTC derivatives market can affect many Americans. Many of us have interests in the corporations, mutual funds, pension funds, insurance companies, municipalities and other entities trading in these instruments."[4]

By saying out loud what we would learn in 2007 and 2008 was the truth, Born drew the ire of some very powerful members of The Club. "[Alan] Greenspan told Brooksley that she essentially didn't know what she was doing and she'd cause a financial crisis," recalled Michael Greenberger, who was a senior director at the Commodity Futures Trading Commission.[5] Alan S. Blinder, a former Federal Reserve board member and an economist at Princeton University added: "Proposals to bring even minimalist regulation were basically rebuffed by Greenspan and various people in the Treasury. I think of him as consistently cheerleading on derivatives."[6] The "various people" Blinder referred to included Robert Rubin. (Among the many companies lobbying against any regulation was Enron, which would use derivatives to construct a phony financial pyramid that would spectacularly collapse.) Ultimately, Rubin's opposition to Born and the role he played in removing Glass-Steagall lead to the rapid growth of derivatives, particularly the credit-default swaps which fueled the 2008 financial crisis.

The attacks against Born had a lot to do with her being outside The Club. As Greenberger put it: "Brooksley was this woman who was not playing tennis with these guys and not having lunch with these guys. There was a little bit of the feeling that this woman was not of Wall Street."[7] This observation says much about how Rubin, and the Wall Street elite, operated and continue to operate. Simply put, members of The Club took care of each other. For example, if bondholders here or abroad were in danger of being wiped out by a currency crisis in, say, Mexico, a few phone calls would secure a bailout to make sure the bondholders did not lose their money. Similarly, if a troublesome regulation was in the way of corporate profits, The Club pulled the right strings and the regulation was gone, all with the ideological rhetorical flourish that the regulation was making the American economy "uncompetitive."

Rubin's "Miracle"

One of the reasons that to this day Robert Rubin remains the critical darling of the mainstream and financial media is that he continues to successfully ride the myth about his role in the economic "miracle" of the 1990s. For nearly fifteen years, both he and Bill Clinton have promoted the mystique of themselves as the dynamic duo of economic geniuses, who, by reducing the deficit they inherited from the Reagan and Bush administrations, ignited a surge in jobs, investment, productivity and wages which transformed the "new" economy. That legend endured even after Clinton left office in 2000. Indeed, Al Gore was roundly criticized for not embracing the Clinton "good times" when he ran for president, a failure that is' often cited for his loss to George W. Bush; in addition, the ensuing two-term economic disaster of the second Bush administration has been routinely compared, by Democrats (and Clinton himself), to the fantastic economic record of the 1990s. Hillary Clinton, during her failed presidential campaign in 2008, regularly wrapped herself in the legacy of her husband's economic record, saying implicitly or explicitly (or having surrogates take up the chore of promoting the spin), that if America chose wisely and tapped her to be the country's next leader, the economic good times would roll once again.

However, there is one thing wrong with the legend of the Clinton-Rubin economic miracle of the 1990s—it isn't true. As economist Dean Baker points out, "The growth burst of the late 1990s had little to do with deficit reduction (at least directly) and had everything to do with two unsustainable bubbles—a stock market bubble and a dollar bubble. The Clinton administration chose to ride the prosperity from these bubbles, even though it should have recognized that this prosperity was artificial, and would inevitably lead to a crash, followed by a painful adjustment process."[8]

These twin bubbles fostered the illusion among many Americans that they were worth a lot of money, despite the fact that their wealth existed only on paper, and did not come from actual wage increases. The result was a Wal-Mart wet-dream: as the high dollar made imports cheap, people snapped up these cheap goods, which fattened the bottom line of companies that trafficked in these products, such as Wal-Mart. At the same time, perceiving themselves to be richer than they actually were thanks to the stock market bubble, and feeling that they were heading towards a comfortable retirement, people saved less. As Baker writes, "With the market rising at double digit rates through the second half of the 1990s, many workers not only assumed that past gains would be enduring, but that this rate of growth would continue. As a result, they saw little reason to save from current income. It is remarkable, that at a time when virtually the entire baby boom cohort was in its peak savings years, the **savings rate hit the lowest levels seen up until that point.** While saving as a share of disposable income averaged 9.6 percent in the seventies, and 9.0 percent in eighties, it averaged just 3.3 percent from 1996 to 2000, hitting 2.3 percent in 2000 itself."[9] [emphasis added] Rather than being an anomaly, the Clinton-Rubin era was simply another link in the three-decade "free market" push, and actually set up the vast financial collapse of 2008, as it came to be accepted wisdom that economic bubbles could be substituted for real wage growth.

"A low probability that things could get considerably worse"
Another reason that the questionable judgments of Rubin have continued to avoid close scrutiny is because we have a set of uninformed people masquerading as journalists. No better example of the lack of depth of understanding among the media—and one of the reasons the traditional press is losing its grip on framing the news—can be found than in the person of Bob Schieffer, one of the "deans" of the national news shows. In the space of less than three months in 2008, Schieffer interviewed Rubin twice on *Face the Nation*, both times in Rubin's capacity as an advisor to then candidate Barack Obama. It is truly illuminating to read the exchanges and see Schieffer absorb the full Rubin, their back-and-forth reflecting the dominant, mainstream and quite narrow view of economics.

During the first interview, on August 3, 2008, Schieffer asked Rubin how he would "sum up the economic system in this country," adding that "some people say we're already in a recession, some say we might be heading toward a depression." Rubin responded that he had "been around markets and economic issues for a long, long time" and while it was now a "very complex, very uncertain time," there was "a low probability that things could get considerably worse."

Schieffer followed up by asking about Rubin about then candidate Obama's proposed economic plan. "He wants to give people what, 1,000 bucks, basically, to help with their energy—with their energy costs? He's going to pay for that how, did you say?" Rubin answered by saying that "Now, different people may have different views about what the pay for ought to be, but he reflects his deeply internalized sense that we must, for the long term, restore sound fiscal conditions after a current decade in which we've had very unsound fiscal policy with, I think, a very great danger to the future of this country." Rubin finished by saying that "Sound fiscal conditions were central to the very good economic conditions of the 1990s, including enormous numbers of new jobs and rising wages at all levels."[10]

On October 26, 2008—just days before the national election— Rubin returned to *Face the Nation* and took part in the following exchange with Schieffer:

SCHIEFFER: The government passed this huge bailout bill. We've seen governments around the world taking actions to ease the financial crisis. Yet if we look at the stock market, none of it seems to be working or making much difference. Is it just too early to tell, Mr. Rubin, or do other things need to be done?

ROBERT RUBIN (Former Treasury Secretary; Senior Economic Advisor, Obama Campaign): Bob, I think actually there has been some change. If you look at the credit markets—which is what really is going to determine what happens to our economy, not the stock market—there was quite a bit of improvement over the last week. But most fundamentally, there has been very strong action, as you say, but I think there is a lot more that we need to do.... But enormous amount has been done, and I think it will take a little time for that to work its way through...But I do think the power of public policy in its entirety, that which has been done plus a large fiscal stimulus and the other kinds of measures we can take, should be able to stem this within a reasonable period of time.[11]

In the first interview in August, Rubin established his bona fides as a person who had been "around markets and economic issues for a long, long time" and again offered the myth, accepted as gospel by the traditional media, about the Clinton-Rubin years of "fiscal discipline" and economic prosperity. However, not once in either interview did Schieffer ask Rubin about the false underpinnings of the Clinton-Rubin era, about the 1990s stock market bubble Rubin oversaw and did nothing to address, about the undoing of basic regulations that might have saved trillions of dollars in wealth from being destroyed in 2008 and, not insignificantly, about Rubin's woeful record at Citigroup, where shareholders suffered losses of more than 70 percent from the time he joined the firm in 1999 until his resignation in early 2009.[12] Nor did Schieffer bother to point out in the October interview that Rubin had been wrong when he predicted in August that there was a "low probability" that the economic crisis would worsen, when, in fact the Dow had plummeted 777 points at the end of September, wiping out $1.2 trillion worth of wealth in one day. Instead, what we got was a classic traditional media show: a surface discussion about politics and policy that never demanded accountability, but was instead a great lesson in obfuscation.

"Nobody was prepared for this"

Despite the constant and ongoing genuflection he continues to receive from the media, the 2008 financial crisis has in fact caused damage to Rubin's most valuable asset, which, as I've tried to show, is not his money, real estate or other investments, but his reputation as an economic guru; a reputation that, once made, has almost never been challenged.

At the end of 2008, Rubin was drawing a lot of flack, given the bailout of Citigroup, and the news that he had earned $115 million at the company (not including stock options) since 1999.[13] That's a lot of money for someone to make whose defense against the collapse of his company, in an extraordinary November 2008 interview with *The Wall Street Journal*, boiled down to: I was not responsible and/or I didn't know. The seer of the markets, the man who had forged the country's economic destiny in the 1990s, whose links to investment banking firms went back three decades, who brought Congressional hearings to a hush as he dispensed advice roundly perceived as The Word From The Mountaintop, and who was one of the leaders of one of the largest banks in the world—in short, the president of The Club—was reduced, apparently, to being an innocent bystander as Cititgroup disintegrated around him. "Under fire for his role in the near-collapse of Citigroup Inc.," the *Journal* reported, "Robert Rubin said its problems were due to the buckling financial system, not its own mistakes, and that his role was peripheral to the bank's main operations even though he was one of its highest-paid officials… 'Nobody was prepared for this,' Mr. Rubin said in an interview."[14] The article also stated that despite the fact that Rubin was involved in the decision of the Citigroup board to ramp up risk-taking in 2004 and 2005, he was "warning publicly that investors were taking too much risk."

Whatever you think of Rubin's tenure at Citigroup, that last statement is simply false, as there is not a single public pronouncement that he made about investors taking on too much risk in the years leading up to the financial crisis of 2008. As a matter of fact, when he was Treasury Secretary, Rubin was well aware of the dangers of leverage and either tried to downplay those dangers or else encouraged people to look the other way. For example, at the World Economic Forum in Davos in January 1999, in a talk that addressed the Asian financial crisis (which, ironically given today's crisis, he called "the most serious financial crisis of the last 50 years"), Rubin said:

> Leverage throughout the international financial system has been substantially reduced over recent months, and that

probably makes the financial system safer today than it was last summer. Without prejudging anything, it does seem to me that this whole question of leverage merits further examination. As a related matter, while I do not believe that hedge funds have been a significant factor in the financial crisis, their activities may well have amplified market movements in some cases for some period of time. I think questions about hedge funds should be addressed, but as part of a broader review of financial institutions generally with respect to leverage, the appropriate scope of prudential regulation, risk management and disclosure.[15]

By acknowledging that leverage had been reduced and that it, by inference, had been a significant factor in the Asian financial crisis, you would think that Rubin would have been similarly warning us in recent years about the leverage of Wall Street firms. Yet, there is no public record of the warnings Rubin claims he made. In fact, if Rubin had learned anything from the Asian crisis, then why did he let Citigroup effectively go down the same leveraged road? Because it was someone else's fault, he told the *Wall Street Journal*, saying that it was the company's "risk-management executives" who were responsible for the problems that Citigroup faced. "The board can't run the risk book of a company," Rubin said, exonerating both himself and his fellow board members. "The board as a whole is not going to have a granular knowledge" of operations.[16] Rubin made this extraordinary statement of ignorance despite the fact that the Journal article said that, "Colleagues deferred to him [Rubin], as the only board member with experience as a trader or risk manager."

Ultimately, Rubin said that the decision by Citigroup to increase risk "followed a presentation to the board by a consultant who said the bank had committed less of the capital on its balance sheet, on a risk-adjusted basis, than competitors."[17] So again, it wasn't the board's fault—a board Rubin sat on at quite a large expense to the company. Instead, it was an unnamed consultant's fault. Despite his status as an economic leader, we are supposed to believe that Rubin was incapable of seeing the economic dangers of increased risk—which he himself had spoken against in reference to the Asian financial crisis.

In the end, the saddest part of Rubin's defense is that he could have done so much more for himself and, more importantly, for the country, if he simply said, "I screwed up." By virtue of his exalted status, he could, in fact, have moved us away from a failed economic vision if he had simply offered up a statement of responsibility. But, it just isn't in his DNA to admit failure—to do so would have punctured the reputation he had worked so hard to build.

New Players, Same Ideology

Though Rubin hasn't been as prominent in the media recently, and currently doesn't have a formal role in the government, his long shadow still casts itself over the nation's economic policy. For example, one of his protégés, Timothy F. Geithner, is now the Secretary of the Treasury, and was largely responsible for committing hundreds of billions of taxpayer dollars to shore up the nation's faltering banking system in 2009. While some analysts and observers chose to paint Geithner's activities in conspiratorial terms, it is far more important to instead see his actions, which protected banking executives and shareholders at the expense of working people, in light of his allegiance to, and shared philosophy with, The Club.

During his tenure as head of the New York Federal Reserve Bank—first among equals in the federal reserve kingdom—Geithner caucused not with regular people or even informed advocates who worked outside the system, but instead exchanged ideas with the very bank executives he was charged to regulate. As *The New York Times* reported in April 2009, Geithner, while serving as head of the New York Federal Reserve, "ate lunch with senior executives from Citigroup, Goldman Sachs and Morgan Stanley at the Four Seasons restaurant or in their corporate dining rooms. He attended casual dinners at the homes of executives like Jamie Dimon, a member of the board of the New York Federal Reserve and the CEO and chairman of JPMorgan Chase."[18] While enjoying these fancy dinners, Geithner apparently did not warn his Clubmates of the impending financial crisis, nor did he step in to restrain the reckless behavior undertaken by the wide circle of people he regularly dined with.

Another Rubin acolyte who is no less influential in the economic stewardship of the country is Lawrence Summers who serves as the chairman of the Council of Economic Advisors for President Obama. Summers has a long history of—how do I put it?—"questionable" views. When he was president of Harvard University, he suggested that the innate difference between men and women explained why women were less successful in math and science.[19] Years before, while wearing his hat as the chief economist for the World Bank, Summers argued that Third World countries would be a proper dumping ground for pollution-causing industries.[20] But, more to the point here, Summers is a product of the groupthink culture of finance in America. He was a key player in the campaign against Brooksley Born, attacking her views because they would "cast the shadow of regulatory uncertainty over an otherwise thriving market, raising risks for the stability and competitiveness of American derivative trading."[21]

Summer's close ties to the financial world have generated a tidy cash return for him as well. As the *Washington Post* reported in April of 2009, "Lawrence H. Summers, one of President Obama's top economic advisers, collected roughly $5.2 million in compensation from hedge fund D.E. Shaw over the past year and was paid more than $2.7 million in speaking fees by several troubled Wall Street firms and other organizations…Financial institutions including JP Morgan Chase, Citigroup, Goldman Sachs, Lehman Brothers and Merrill Lynch paid Summers for speaking appearances in 2008. Fees ranged from $45,000 for a November 12 Merrill Lynch appearance to $135,000 for an April 16 visit to Goldman Sachs, according to his disclosure form."[22]

While cashing in personally on his deep ties certainly raises ethical questions, the larger point is that Summers, like Geithner, inhabit the world of The Club, and thus it is hard to see how either of them can, or are even willing, to fundamentally change the rules of the financial game in this country. Taken at its least conspiratorial level, consider this: one could argue that the financial crisis that rocked the world in 2008 and 2009 showed that the Citigroup model of finance—where massive, multi-national banks dominate the landscape, searching the world for schemes like credit-default swaps that can return huge profits (and cause massive losses, as well)—is a fundamental danger to a healthy economy. As a result, we would be better off returning to an economy where regional and community banks rule the credit markets, caring more about catering to mom-and-pop small businesses or the homeowner down the street, rather than a trader at some distant financial institution halfway around the world. However, what are the chances that either Summers or Geithner would lead the charge for such a change, a change which would threaten The Club?

3.The Stock Option Scam

In this chapter (and the three that follow), I will discuss some of the specific ways that the CEO Robber Barons—using the rhetoric of the "free market" and the support of their accomplices in The Club— have looted this country, in the process hoarding vast sums of money for themselves while leaving regular Americans with ever smaller paychecks and an ever shrinking standard of living.

Let's start with stock options. The argument is simple: by making each employee a shareholder in the company, everyone—including management—will work together toward the shared goal of making the company successful. This philosophy works on two basic psychological levels: by enhancing the notion of a society where, when you succeed, you are rewarded with a piece of the pie that you helped bake, as well as burnishing the idea that everyone can enjoy the success of the "free market" by becoming a stakeholder in the market. Unfortunately, as we shall see, the theory of stock option incentive exists only in the world of free market fantasy. In the real world, the theory has proven to be a complete sham—unless, of course, you are the CEO of the company.

During the 1950s, stock options became a popular form of executive payment, as companies used them as a cost-effective method to compensate executives. However, as the value of the dollar declined in the 1970s and stock prices were flat, the popularity of stock options waned and companies shifted to performance-based rewards for executives, which were paid out over a fixed amount of time based on the meeting of company goals. This type of option was viewed by executives as more of a long-term retirement package rather than a quick way to make money.

In the 1980s, as the stock market soared in value, stock options again became popular, and the era of the super-sized option was born. With stock prices becoming the ultimate benchmark of corporate performance, shareholders now wanted CEOs to dedicate their efforts to increasing share price, rather than focusing on the overall health of the company.[1] Felix Rohatyn, an investment banker famous for his role in preventing the bankruptcy of New York City during the 1970s, recalls "sitting on the boards of some large companies at the time [1980s] pressured by institutional investors who demanded changes in compensation packages aimed at greater stock interests for management and lower cash payouts. That meant more stock options."[2] As stock prices continued to climb in the 1990s and into the new millennium, CEOs were increasing rewarded solely on the value of their company's stock, essentially severing the connection between compensation and executive performance. CEOs could now become extremely wealthy with little, if any, responsibility to the company's employees. The scene was now set for a small minority to benefit at the expense of the working majority.

A quick refresher course on how stock options work. A company grants their CEO an option to buy say 1,000 shares of his company at $40 a share on October 1, 2009. A year later, on October 1, 2010—typically, a CEO has to wait a full year to exercise his options—the stock price is now $50 per share. But, unlike the regular guy in the street, on October 1, 2010, the CEO can still buy the stock at $40 a share—that's the "option." Thus, the CEO has immediately made himself $10,000: $10 extra on the profit between the $40 per share on his option and the going price on October 1, 2010 of $50 per share. Of course, these options are usually given out in much bigger chunks than 1,000 shares—millions of options on occasion—so you can see how a CEO can really make a financial killing.

Probably one of the best observers of the stock options' scam is Graef "Bud" Crystal. Now semi-retired and living north of San Francisco, Crystal was once one of the country's premier compensation consultants—the outside fixers that CEOs and their boards bring in to give their robbery of shareholders a veneer of respectability. According to Crystal, the original notion of CEO compensation was simple: you pitched your pay level to that of other CEOs. But that notion didn't last long. "In 1970, one CEO hired me and said, 'we don't have a bonus plan and do we need one?'" recalls Crystal. "I did the study and I went back to the CEO and said 'yes you do need a bonus plan. But we have a problem area. You are making $150,000-a year and the problem is that the $150,000 is equal to the salary and the bonus to what your competitors are paying so we have to cut your pay to $100,000-a-year and then we can put in a bonus.'" Crystal laughs. "It was like a scene from *The Exorcist* where ice formed on the windows…he started arguing about the findings and he finally said 'let me say this to you this way: who do you think is paying your bills anyway?' I replied, 'If I recall correctly the checks were drawn on the corporate account, not your personal account so the shareholders are paying me, not you.' The meeting ended quite quickly."[3]

One of Crystal's early clients was the H.J. Heinz Company. "In 1973, at first, the CEO was in a non-descript building nestled in a big factory. I would come to meet with him, and I would be assaulted by the smells when I walked in," Crystal remembers. "I observed real work going on, their testing lab was there." Then, says Crystal, the CEO retired, and was succeeded in 1979 by Anthony J.F. O'Reilly, a very flamboyant, bon vivant Irishman. "He was a renowned rugby star of his time, handsome, smart. He didn't take kindly to his little office building. U.S. Steel had built the largest building in Pittsburgh and was just going bankrupt. O'Reilly decided he wanted that space [in the U.S. steel building]. In there, you would ride in a very fancy elevator, you'd get out on the 60th floor and you'd have to almost use a machete to get through the thick carpet and everyone would be speaking in hushed tones and no one but the secretaries made less than a million dollars a year. They didn't care what the workers were paid because they never saw the workers."

O'Reilly liked to shower himself, and his adoring fans, with corporate excess. A September 1997 *Business Week* story captured his style of management:

On August 10th, some 500 guests of H.J. Heinz Chairman and Chief Executive Anthony J.F. O'Reilly gathered under chandeliers in a mammoth white pavilion set up at the swanky Leopardstown horse-racing track outside Dublin. More than half were flown in from around the world, put up at Ireland's finest hotels, and feted at a lavish three-day bash. Guests included H.J. Heinz Co. executives and directors, Wall Street analysts, and assorted politicians, tycoons, and friends. In recent years, Paul Newman, William Kennedy Smith, and the CEOs of PepsiCo, Sara Lee, and Clorox have joined in the fun.

From a gala ball at O'Reilly's own Georgian mansion to the main event, the Heinz 57 Phoenix Stakes, no expense was spared. And with Heinz picking up the tab, O'Reilly was clearly the star of the show. Arriving last to the pre-race luncheon, he and his wife, Chryss, stepped gingerly from a blue Bentley. As they made their entrance, O'Reilly began working the room, offering handshakes, jokes, and whispered asides with a politician's natural ease. "When he walks into the marquee, the whole place comes alive," recalls a recent guest. "Short of a U.S. President's arrival, I've never seen anything like it."[4]

In the six years prior to 1997 (during five of which *Business Week* ranked him as one of the five CEOs giving shareholders the least value for their money), O'Reilly pocketed $182.9 million, mainly as a result of massive stock options. In 1996 alone, he received a grant of 750,000 shares—646,800 more than his nearest peer, Campbell Soup Chairman David Johnson, had gotten over the previous seven years combined.[5]

However, O'Reilly was one-upped in 1996 by then Walt Disney CEO Michael Eisner, who, according to Crystal (who was Disney's compensation consultant at the time), received "an enormous grant of 24 million shares in a single day, the largest ever seen then. I said that if you are going to get this grant, we need to put some teeth in it, we should set the strike price much higher than the market price so you have to make quite a bit of progress to make a buck. I pushed and shoved and the compromise was: he'd get 15 million where the market price was equal to the strike price, 3 million shares where the strike price was set 25 percent higher than the market, 3 million where the strike would be 50 percent higher than the market; and the last 3 million share where it was set 100 percent higher than the market price."

At the time, Crystal says that the value of that one-time grant was $170 million. "Those numbers went into everyone's comparative databases, including car companies and others that were not even in the same [movie] industry," he recalls with amazement. "I could almost hear the consultants calling up and asking, 'Where are the compensation committees?' and, if they were told they were on the way to the plane, they would say, 'Stop the plane. Michael Eisner just got this huge grant and you are way behind.'" To help mitigate the risk to Michael Eisner—the risk of having a package that was worth $170 million—the board of Disney agreed that the premium priced options (the ones Eisner got that were set above the level of the market price on the day the options were granted) would exist for 15 years, not 10 years as was typical.

"Sitting Back on the Roadside"
The obscene options offered to CEOs like O'Reilly and Eisner in the mid-1990s established an arms race in compensation among

corporate executives, particularly in the area of stock options. As a result, the stock option haul for the top five executives at the largest 1,500 U.S. firms went from $2.4 billion in 1992 to $18 billion in 2000, an increase of 650 percent. In addition, by 2000, executives had also accumulated $80 billion from the stockpile of options they owned but hadn't yet cashed in. That number was a ten-fold increase from 1992.[6] Yet those figures seem like chump change compared to the current numbers. Using the *New York Times* annual CEO survey that I mentioned in the introduction to the book, in 2007 alone, the top 200 CEOs rang up $1.3 billion in stock option gains and another $646 million in stock award gains.

Based on classical economic theory, there could only be two reasons for this rapid increase in CEO pay: a decline in supply, or a rise in demand. On the supply side, the market's cup was overflowing, and the elite business schools were churning out graduates like crazy. And demand? For every company that had been formed or split into more than one part, there were hundreds of companies that were merging or going out of business. Citigroup, for example, grew partly through a merger of Travelers Insurance, Salamon Brothers and eventually Smith Barney. Theoretically then, demand—and pay— should have either been declining for CEOs, or at the very least, remained stable. Then why was it going up so dramatically? Crystal sums it up: "It was a phony market driven by phony numbers."

The phoniness of the exploding CEO market was exposed in the book, *In the Company of Owners,* published in 2003. The book's authors, Joseph Blasi, Douglas Kruse and Aaron Bernstein, found no correlation between the size of stock options and corporate performance. "The companies whose executives took more had no better returns in the following three years than those that took less," they wrote. "Worse, firms whose corporate chieftains were most likely to take a bigger share had subpar performance to begin with. Since the extra ownership made no difference, the shareholders with the greediest CEOs were just throwing good money after bad. The relationship held true regardless of the size of the corporation, as measured either by its market value or how many employees it had."They concluded by stating that, "Overall it seems clear that options have been seriously misused as a tool for motivating executives. CEOs have taken much more wealth than they can justify, and they've shared too little with average employees if the goal is to create a more entrepreneurial workplace. Corporate America's CEOs cut themselves and an elite group of executives and others employees in on an unbelievably lucrative ride, and left almost everyone else in their companies sitting back on the roadside."[7]

Backdating

While, true to the "free market" myth, stock options did stimulate some amazing creativity among CEOs, unfortunately that creativity wasn't used to enhance corporate performance. Instead, many CEOs came up with new and creative ways to pump up the value of their stock options even further, using techniques such as backdating, re-pricing and reloading.

Let's begin with backdating. How much would you give if you could buy a ticket and chose the winning numbers of the lottery—after the drawing was over? That is essentially the upshot of the backdating of stock options. Here is how it works: if you are the head honcho at a company, you are allowed to pick the date and price of your stock options after you have seen how low your company's stock went during a given year. So, if you already had an option at $40 per share and today's price is $50 per share, but that $10 per share profit is not enough for you, you have the board date the option back six months, when the stock was at $30 per share. You have now doubled your profit to $20 per share.

The most amazing part of this whole scheme is that backdating can be done legally. If the company did not forge any documents, reflected the change in earnings from the year the option date is reset (because if a CEO is given an option, it's an expense the company will have to pay for and, therefore, it has to be part of the corporate bottom line) and informed the shareholders, then it is all legal. Unfortunately, the audacity of greed was so pervasive that many CEOs, in order to make even more money, often engaged in illegal backdating maneuvers. Through March 2007, over 250 companies had "announced internal investigations, SEC inquiries, or Justice Department subpoenas" related to backdating, while 60 companies had "already taken $5.2 billion in charges to correct backdating."[8]

Among the companies involved in backdating was Barnes and Noble, our friendly chain bookstore serving espresso and intellectual stimulation, which announced on April 4, 2007 that it would take a $23 million hit—but only after a shareholder lawsuit, and investigations by the Securities and Exchange Commission and the Department of Justice forced the company to come clean. More recently, in May 2009, James J. Treacy, the former president and chief operating officer of Monster Worldwide, which owns the online job search site Monster.com, was convicted of "conspiracy and securities fraud in a plot to improperly backdate millions of dollars in stock-options awards." According to the *Wall Street Journal*, "Prosecutors had alleged that Mr. Treacy reaped more than $24 million in a scheme in which he and others 'gamed the system' in order to make millions off stock options from the company."[9]

KB Home, the home builder, shoved its Chairman and CEO Bruce Karatz out the door in November 2006 after a review found that the stock option grants he had received had been dated at a suspiciously low level and that Karatz had backdated his own options. Karatz eventually agreed to forfeit $13 million that he would have made on the options—and the company took a $41.1 million hit to its bottom line when it had to "restate" its annual filings. In May 2009, Karatz was indicted on "multiple counts of fraud and other charges in connection with the alleged backdating of stock-option grants."[10]) The backdating scheme began, according to the fraud indictment, after Karatz tried in 1998 "to get board approval for a plan to grant himself one million stock options at far-below-market prices." After failing to convince the board to go along with his plan, Karatz allegedly ordered "underlings to look back over stock trading to select a date on which the stock was very low." The SEC also said that Karatz continued to backdate options even after the Sarbanes-Oxley Act of 2002 "tightened financial-reporting rules for executive stock-option grants."[11] Karatz's greed was so out-of-control that he had to cheat and lie even after making more money than most people could spend in a lifetime: he collected more than $227 million in compensation from 2000 to 2005[12], including $155.9 million in 2005 alone.[13]

In a celebrated case, Apple appeared to be awash in backdating seaminess—touching even the CEO of the company, Steve Jobs, who would end up skating free-and-clear, with a cloud over his head but no penalties because an "internal" company probe found that while Jobs knew of the backdating, he did not benefit from the incidents. Not so lucky were Apple's former general counsel, Nancy Heinen, and former CFO Fred Anderson: on April 24, 2007, the SEC filed civil charges against the two for their alleged involvement in the backdating scandal. Mr. Anderson wound up doing what a lot of miscreants do, and what the government lets them do: he made a deal without admitting any wrongdoing, paying about $3.5 million in "disgorgement fees."[14]

However, the granddaddy of all backdating scams was pulled off by William McGuire, the former CEO and Chairman of the Board of UnitedHealth Group Inc., the nation's second largest health care company. Dr. McGuire treated the company as his own private piggy bank, as, by the end of 2005, he had piled up stock options worth an astounding $1.6 billion. According to the *Wall Street Journal*, McGuire "got an enormous grant in three parts that—after adjustment for later stock splits—came to 14.6 million options…The 1999 grant was dated the very day UnitedHealth stock hit its low for the year. Grants to Dr. McGuire in 1997 and 2000 were also dated on the day with those years' single lowest closing price. A grant in 2001 came near the bottom of a sharp stock dip. In all, the odds of such a favorable pattern occurring by chance would be one in 200 million or greater."[15] It turned out that the overwhelming number of the 44 million (split-adjusted) UnitedHealth options that McGuire received were backdated illegally, which forced McGuire to shell out a record $468 million in penalties in December 2007—of course, without actually having to admit he did anything wrong; he only had to "disgorge" his dough. The deal was the first one made under a new law that deprived "corporate executives of their stock sale profits and bonuses earned while their companies were misleading investors."[16] Like Karatz, it wasn't as if McGuire was poor—in the time he ran UnitedHealth, on top of his stock options (and, one would assume, very generous expense accounts) he was paid $530 million.[17]

Though McGuire's troubles with the SEC ended, the company he scammed continued to be harmed by his actions. In July 2008, already beset by industry troubles, UnitedHealth had to agree to settle a series of shareholder suits for the tidy sum of more than $900 million.[18] As for McGuire, he was allowed to keep about $800 million worth of his stock options.

Arthur Levitt, a former chairman of the Securities and Exchange Commission, believes that backdating "represents the ultimate in greed. It is stealing, in effect. It is ripping off shareholders in an unconscionable way."[19] A study conducted by M. P. Narayanan, Cindy A. Schipani and H. Nejat Seyhun—business professors at the University of Michigan—supports Levitt's contention, showing how backdating hurts companies and costs shareholders. "The upper bound of managerial benefit derived from these illegal practices averages about three million dollar per firm over a five-year period," the study says. "In contrast, when these practices become public, the damages borne by the shareholders averages about $500 million per firm. Hence, our evidence suggests that managerial theft is not a zero-sum game, but involves huge dead-weight losses for the shareholders."[20]

Similarly, a second study conducted by Narayanan and Seyhun—which looked at 605,106 option grants reported by all managers in all publicly listed companies between 1992 and 2002—showed that "if [the] grant date is back-dated by 20 days, executives receiving large grants (500,000 shares or greater) increase the value of their option compensation by about 10%. By conservative estimates, this is equivalent to a windfall of $0.7 million per grant."[21] Another study conducted by Narayanan and Seyhun, which looked at a larger set of stock option grants in a shorter period of time—638,757 option grant filings between August 29, 2002, and December 31, 2004—found the same scam underway. "Our results show that if grant date is back-dated by 30 days, executives receiving large grants (500,000 shares or greater) increase the value their option compensation by about 8%. By conservative estimates, this is equivalent to a windfall of $1.2 million for a manager receiving a grant of one million options."[22]

Re-pricing and Reloading

Let's turn now to the second stock options scam, known as re-pricing. Say you are a CEO, and your stock options are set at $40 per share. But, you do such a poor job that your company's stock falls to $10 a share. Rather than fire you because of poor performance, your sycophant board of directors throws you a life preserver: they set the price—re-price—your stock options to $5 per share. Now you can exercise your options and still make $5 per share on the sale of each one. With a few millions options in the bank, you can still pocket a substantial sum—without having to account for the company's pathetic performance under your watch. Essentially, re-pricing removes any risk on the CEO's behalf by ensuring that even if the company's stock price plummets—a possible consequence of an inept CEO—he is still able to turn the options into a substantial profit. Basically, it's like flipping a coin—heads the CEO wins, tails the CEO wins. In either case, it is the shareholders and the workers who lose.

Here is an outlandish example of the re-pricing scam, as reported by *The Wall Street Journal* in 2006: "An even more extreme example of re-pricing occurred after such regulations when PMC-Sierra Inc.'s stock plummeted to below $10 a share after previously holding values up to $245 a piece. From 2002 to 2003 the company re-priced 1.6 millions options for CEO Robert Bailey, cutting the executing cost to $5.95 from approximately $52.38. Such drastic re-pricing allowed Bailey to more comfortably deal with the dramatic drop in stock prices, unlike the rest of the company's investors."[23]

And, last but not least, let us ponder the third stock options scam, known as "re-loading." Say a CEO owns 10,000 shares of stock in his company and also has 10,000 options, which he got for a strike price of $10. Two years later, the stock is up to $20. So, his options have earned him $100,000. To lock in some profit, the CEO takes 5,000 of the shares he already owns and exercises his 10,000 options. Those options are then converted into regular shares—and the board of directors "reloads" his options pool with another 5,000 options (equal to the number of shares the CEO used to buy the other options pool), set at the new market price of $20. When all these machinations are complete, the CEO has 15,000 shares and an additional new pool of 5,000 options. He has also made a profit and is poised to make even more money if the price of the shares goes up. (By the way, this little gift is not available to the average company shareholder).

In the final tally, the lust for stock option riches has damaged numerous companies and harmed countless people, mainly regular workers. In their desire for quick, easy money, many CEOs made decisions that inflated the stock price of their companies in the short-term—sometimes by illegally manipulating financial statements to artificially boost the corporate bottom line. In the long-term, the quest for stock options also led to CEOs to make decisions that had devastating effects on their companies, including the firing of workers and the closing down of factories, which the stock market, in all its wisdom, often interpreted as good for a company's bottom line, even if it was not so good for the people who, for the benefit of inflating the CEO's paycheck, were suddenly out of a job.

In addition to hurting regular employees, stock options have also fleeced shareholders, albeit in a more subtle way. Going back to the 1970s, corporate executives didn't have to show a stock option as an expense as long as the option was set at the price the stock was at on the day the option was given. Therefore, companies never had to inform shareholders of the true cost of CEO compensation. This made the board of directors look like geniuses, as they could retain the CEO at a certain salary, without disclosing the hidden riches the CEO would pocket down the road. While that rule was changed in 2004 so that shareholders could get a more accurate reading of the financial commitment they would be laying out to the CEO in the future, by then, the damage had been done.

4. Vodka and Penises

Vodka spouting from a penis must be a sight to see. And, vodka spraying from the penis of a replica of Michelangelo's David must be something even more amazing to behold. Indeed, it is quite unusual to find the words "Vodka," "Penis" and "Michelangelo" linked together in the same sentence.

For that unique string of words, we can thank Dennis Kozlowski and, one assumes, the great love he had for his wife. In 2000, Kozlowski decided that his second wife, Karen Mayo, deserved a top-of-the-line party in honor of her fortieth birthday. So he flew seventy-five guests to the Hotel Cala di Volpe in Sardinia, Italy, where the privileged invitees played golf and tennis, ate fine food, listened to a performance by the singer Jimmy Buffett (who was paid a fee of $250,000 to appear) and enjoyed a birthday cake in the shape of a woman's breasts festooned with sparklers on top.[1] However, the defining extravagance of the party was an ice sculpture of Michelangelo's David featuring vodka spouting from its penis. I wonder what people thought as they stood watching such a spectacle. Did they think it was funny? Erotic? Artistic?

At the same time, I wonder if anyone at the party even gave a passing thought about who had paid for the over-the-top festivities. I suppose that a man should be allowed to throw a lavish birthday party for his wife, even if the excess and bad taste border on the bizarre. And, if you want to foot the bill—in this case, $2 million—

then heck, knock yourself out.

But Dennis Kozlowski had a small problem, which ended up being quite a large problem—the money for the party came out of the coffers of Tyco, Inc., the company for which he served as chief executive officer. And, even though his pay had soared from $8.8 million in 1997 to $67 million in 1998 to a startling $170 million in 1999, ranking him second in CEO pay that year, the party wasn't the only thing that Kozlowski had dipped into the company's coffers to finance. Among the items that Kozlowski bought for himself on Tyco's dime included:

- $6,000 shower curtain
- $15,000 dog umbrella stand
- $6,300 sewing basket
- $17,100 traveling toilette box
- $2,200 gilt metal wastebasket
- $2,900 coat hangers
- Two sets of sheets for $5,960
- $1,650 appointment book
- $445 pincushion[2]

However, the party for his wife and the stuff listed above added up to mere pocket change compared to Kozlowski's large-scale looting, which included borrowing $61.7 million worth of unauthorized, interest-free loans from Tyco, of which he repaid only $21.7 million. (Kozlowski "forgave" himself $19.4 million worth of the loans—an act of charity his board of directors never authorized—and moved an additional $20.5 million to other loan accounts he held with the company.)[3]

What did those "loans" pay for? A $29.8 million mansion in Boca Raton, Florida; a $7 million co-op in New York City; a second apartment on Fifth Avenue which cost $16.8 million (with an additional $14 million thrown in to furnish and upgrade the apartment); a rare 1930s vintage yacht that carried a $15 million price tag; a raft of art—including "Fleurs et Fruit" by Renior and a $5 million Monet—that totaled about $20 million, which Kozlowski evaded paying New York State sales tax on; and $1.5 million so that his wife Karen could open a restaurant near their Boca Raton home.[4] Kozlowski also generously made contributions to charity and non-profit causes—not out of his pocket, but from the company's funds—another unauthorized spending spree that cost $43 million. He also bought off members of his inner circle so that they would keep quiet about his activities, paying 51 Tyco employees $56 million in bonuses—and $39 million more to pay the taxes on those bonuses—none of which was approved by Tyco's board.[5] In total, Kozlowski misappropriated approximately $400 million worth of company funds.

In June 2005, Kozlowski and a co-defendant, former Tyco chief financial officer Mark Swartz, were convicted on all but one of twenty-three counts of larceny, fraud, conspiracy and falsifying business records. Three months later, Kozlowksi was sentenced to between 8 1/3 and 25 years in prison—a sentence he would serve not in a minimum-security federal prison, but in a far less inviting lock-up in the New York State penal system.[6]

Kozlowski's conviction did not end the pain for Tyco, however, as his illegal spending eventually wound up costing the company an additional three billion dollars. That was the price tag for the settlement of a lawsuit brought by shareholders who sued Tyco claiming that "the company's leadership [had] engaged in a massive accounting fraud scheme."[7] Understandably, shareholders were quite upset that Tyco had lost $90 billion in market value in 2002, partly in response to fatal strategic decisions that Kolowski had made while pursuing his personal looting of the company.

While Dennis Kozlowski may be the poster child for excessive greed, the characteristics he manifested represented a personality trait common among a certain infamous group of elite CEOs, including Bernard Ebbers of WorldCom, Kenneth Lay and Jeffrey Skilling of Enron, John J. Rigas of Adelphi and Gary Winnick of Global Crossing. The trait that these men shared was the belief that they were the most important, indispensable part of their respective companies, and therefore were entitled to obscene financial rewards, legal or otherwise. A December 2002 Business Week article on the greed of Kozlowski summed it up for all these CEOs: "Abraham Zeleznik, a psychoanalyst and professor emeritus at Harvard Business School, suggests that Kozlowski was undone by a rampant sense of entitlement: 'By entitlement I mean an aspect of a narcissistic personality who comes to believe that he and the institution are one' and thus 'that he can take what he wants when he wants it.'[8]

While you could simply blame narcissism—a latent trait that all of us carry to some degree—for the greed of these CEOs, the narcissistic personality only explodes into full view when those who strongly possess the trait are put into environments where they are praised without question or criticism. In the case of the aforementioned CEOs, it was the press—especially the business press— which, by plastering magazine covers with photos of these supposed God-like conquerors of the market and writing articles that praised their genius at making money, placed these CEOs high on their narcissistic pedestals. In virtually every circumstance of illegal behavior, the corporate criminal was at some point the toast of the business world thanks to a public relations fellatio applied by fawning journalists seduced by access to powerful executives.

"All in all, this was a solid quarter for WorldCom"

Bernard Ebbers was another self-absorbed CEO who gobbled up companies in the telecommunications industry to eventually create a behemoth called WorldCom. At its height, WorldCom generated $40 billion a year in revenue, reaching its pinnacle in 1998 when it bought MCI for $47 billion, creating MCI WorldCom. The company spanned six continents, connecting 60,000 buildings with more than 90,000 miles of land and undersea fiber optic cables.

In October 2000, Ebbers was very bullish on the company's financial results, making this statement to analysts:

We are pleased with our industry-leading incremental revenue growth of $1.1 billion this quarter. Commercial services revenues of $6.4 billion is up 19% year-over-year. And while we continued to hit bumps in the road in the dial-up Internet business, we did produce good results in dedicated Internet and our consumer services businesses. All in all, this was a solid quarter for WorldCom.[9]

There was only only problem with Ebber's statement: it was a lie. Not just in this instance, but, repeatedly, over the course of two years, Ebbers would lie to investors and analysts, manipulating figures to cover up any shortfall in expectations on how his company was performing. As a result, he helped generate an $11 billion accounting fraud, the largest in history.[10] (Ebbers would again make his mark in financial history when WorldCom filed for bankruptcy in 2002 to the tune of $107 billion—the largest bankruptcy ever at the time.)[11]

Ebbers did all this for one reason, and one reason only: to artificially inflate WorldCom's stock in order to make sure that his wealth kept growing. In 1999, he ranked as one of the 200 richest Americans, worth $1.4 billion, almost all of it a reflection of World-Com's stock price. However, with outstanding loans to Bank of America reaching hundreds of millions of dollars, Ebbers could feel his financial world—with his 60-foot yacht and private jet, among other goodies—slowly coming apart. His companion in crime, Scott D. Sullivan, WorldCom's chief financial officer, helped to hide the company's financial reality from the rest of the world so that he too could maintain hold of his opulent lifestyle, which included building a 24,000 square foot mega-mansion in Boca Raton, Florida, which would have held a private art gallery, private theater and lagoon (he would have to sell this home as part of his plea-bargain for a lighter, five-year jail term). When the Ebbers-Sullivan scheme was finally uncovered, WorldCom was forced to announce in June 2002 that it would restate its financial statements. Within days, the price of the company's stock cratered by more than 90 percent, resulting in a loss to shareholder value of more than $2 billion.[12]

That Ebbers would be convicted of numerous felonies in March 2005 and be sentenced to twenty-five years in prison provided little solace to the thousands of people who had lost their jobs and/or life savings because of his crimes. "I represent the common man... the working professional...and the average investor that has suffered untold human carnage financially, personally, and professionally as a result of the criminal activities of Bernard Ebbers and his co-conspirators," ex-WorldCom employee Henry Bruen told the court during Ebber's trial. Bruen said that he lost $800,000, including his home, and, at the time, told the court that he was living with his parents.[13]

Beyond the personal devastation to WorldCom workers and investors, Ebbers' crimes imposed a cost on society in ways that are rarely toted up. For example, rivals in the telecommunications industry like AT&T and Verizon made decisions on prices and other competitive matters based on the profits reported by WorldCom. But since WorldCom's business profile was based on deceit and phony numbers, competitors were effectively boxing at economic shadows. At the very least, thousands of workers at WorldCom's competitors may have lost their jobs solely because of cuts imposed to lower costs to match false profits. In turn, those unemployed workers had to draw down on savings, put off expenditures on health care, college, or other basic needs, as well as live off unemployment insurance—all costs that ripple through the economy, but are hard to total up.

The Family that Steals Together...

There must have been something about the telecommunications industry in the early part of the decade, as Bernard Ebbers' looting was matched by the deeds of the Rigas family—father John and his two sons, Tim and Michael—who turned Adelphia Communications, a national cable giant, into their own personal ATM machine. One month after Adelphia filed for bankruptcy in 2002, the three Rigas' were arrested and charged with "one of the most extensive financial frauds ever to take place at a public company"—a fraud that led to the collapse of the company, which was crushed by $18.6 billion in debt.[14]

According to the SEC indictment, the Rigas' "fraudulently excluded billions of dollars in liabilities from [Adelphia's] consolidated financial statements by hiding them on the books of off-balance sheet affiliates"; "falsified operations statistics and inflated earnings to meet Wall Street's expectations"; and used corporate funds for stock purchases "and the acquisition of luxury condominiums in New York and elsewhere."[15] The families' extravagances were mind-boggling: millions spent on private flights for shopping sprees or trips to Africa; a $150 million loan to prop up a professional hockey team owned by John Rigas; $13 milliion to build a golf course (and more money to pay for assorted other golf memberships); $3 million to finance a movie made by Ellen Rigas, John's daughter; as well as countless other luxuries.[16]

To keep all this hidden, the Rigas' kept two sets of books; while Adelphia would report to the public one set of numbers—say, claiming in one quarter that it had maintained growth to keep pace with its chief competitor, Comcast, when in fact its actual growth was far lower—internally, it kept numbers that told the real story.[17] In July 2004, John Rigas and his son Timothy were each found guilty on eighteen felony counts of fraud and conspiracy; they would later be sentenced, respectively, to 15 and 20 year prison terms.[18] The jury could not reach a verdict on Michael Rigas, who ultimately pleaded guilty in November 2005 to making a false entry in a company record in order to avoid a lengthy jail term had he been found guilty in a new trial on more serious charges.[19]

For the most part, the Rigas' thievery was made possible by a system run by people who chose not to look closely at what was going on at Adelphia, and who, in fact, profited from the web of deceit and financial manipulation that the family wove. "The failed gatekeeper is a lesson you take away from all of these cases," remarked Steve Thel, a Fordham University law professor who specializes in security fraud. "Auditors who didn't want to lose a client, bankers who were doing a ton of deals—there was a sense in our society that people who have a lot of money are supposed to have it."[20] Chief among the willing enablers of Adelphia were commercial banks, who lent the Rigas's a total of $5.6 billion, and in particular their investment banking divisions, which reaped very large fees to make the deals happen. It's worth pointing out that the list of banks that lent the money to Adelphia included Citigroup and Bank of America, two of the banks that were caught knee-deep in oiling the debt driven mortgage asset bubble that fueled the 2008 financial crisis. These banks, along with more than thirty others, including J.P. Morgan Chase and Wachovia, as well as Adelphia's accounting firm, Deloitte & Touche, would end up paying $455 million to settle a massive investor lawsuit—but, of course, none of the defendants, who stood by and aided the fraud, admitted any guilt in settling the case, nor would any heads roll at those institutions whose leaders drained their own shareholder money to patch up a very costly mistake.[21]

Tikkun Olam Bespoiled

Another corporate hustler was Gary Winnick, the CEO of Global Crossing from 1997 to 2002. Winnick founded the company—which he incorporated in Bermuda to avoid paying U.S. taxes—in order to build fiber optic networks. Eventually, the company connected 200 cities in 27 countries via 100,000 miles of fiber optic cables. At one point in 2000, Global Crossing' stock reached $64 a share, giving the company a market value of about $47 billion—bigger than such brand names as McDonald's and CBS. Not surprisingly, Winnick was lauded as a wunderkind in the financial press; in April 1999, *Forbes* splashed his mug across its cover with the headline: "Getting Rich at the Speed of Light."

By 2002, however, Global Crossing's shares were worth 15 cents and the company was in bankruptcy—but not before Winnick made more than $700 million on stock options, including $123 million just shortly before the company collapsed.[22] (Winnick also had close ties to high-level Democratic Party officials, including then Democratic National Committee chairman Terry McAuliffe, who pocketed $18 million from an initial investment of $100,000 in Global Crossing).[23] While Winnick claimed at the time that he was just the victim of a market gone south, investigators would later discover that Global Crossing was using swap transactions, a highly complex scheme which involve at least two companies exchanging the same amount of assets or financial commitments, with the end result being that neither company really increases its value by making some new product or building a new system. Though Winnick and other executives from Global Crossing testified before Congress in 2002 that the swaps were based on "strong business cases," in reality, swap transactions are made for the sole purpose of booking deals that appear to increase revenues, particularly at the end of a financial quarter, which, in turn, can temporarily boost the share price of a company.[24] The swap transactions that Global Crossing engaged in helped increase Winnick's wealth, and, despite his claims of ignorance, it is inconceivable that he did not understand the purpose behind such financial sleight of hand.

In addition, Congressional investigators would later determine that Winnick knew as early as 2000 that Global Crossing was not the darling of Wall Street that everyone thought it was. In a memo written in June 2000, Global Crossing's CEO, Leo Hindery, warned Winnick that the future was dire. "The resplendently colored salmon going up river to spawn, at the end of our journey our niche is going to die rather than live and prosper…The stock market can be fooled, but not forever, and it is fundamentally insightful and always unforgiving of being misled…Without looking like we are shaking our bootie all over the world, sell ourselves quickly to whichever of the six possible acquirors offer our shareholders the highest value." This information was not shared with outside investors.[25]

Though he was never indicted for any crimes, Winnick did end up paying millions of dollars to settle suits by shareholders who felt they had been defrauded, including two large employee pension funds that had lost $110 million. One worker, Janet Mahoney, a former call center director, lost almost $80,000; $35,000 in severance pay and $45,000 in retirement funds that she had invested in company stock. While she was getting a few dollars back because of the settlement, referring to Winnick, she said, "Meantime, he walks away with $738 million. Justice is ridiculous."[26] And while Winnick could continue to pad around his Bel-Air mansion, "The severance owed was not Monopoly money to anybody in this room. It was a mortgage payment. It was electricity, water, gas, food," said Adriene Ragland, a former employee who spoke out at a large meeting of former Global Crossing workers. David Archer, another former employee who had directed the company's global advertising, saw his life change because of Winnick's actions. "The employees of Global Crossing who were severed from a company got... gave... got three days notice that their health benefits were being cut off. The loss of severance was a shock to me. It forced me to... my house is up for sale. I'm going to have to simplify my life." Archer recalled Winnick using company money for personal needs, including spending $14,000 to fly to a golf tournament: "Here was a situation where a senior executive of the company was not taking a customer, but was spending company money to bring him and his son-in-law to the Ryder Cup. And that... that is that kind... and nobody thought twice about it, and it was okay."[27]

In the ultimate irony, the opening paragraph on the website of the Winnick Foundation, which Winnick and his wife established in the early 1980s to support health care research, children's literacy and religious tolerance, reads in part, "According to Gary Winnick, the Hebrew phrase 'tikkun olam'—which means repairing the world—is the guiding principle behind every dollar donated to support programs."[28] Rather than repairing the world, Winnick's dollars ended up destroying the lives of many of the people who worked for him.

How exactly does Enron make its money?
The name that has become most synonymous with corporate en-

richment, illegality and failure is Enron. In the same way that "Watergate" has become shorthand for political corruption, "just like Enron" has became a signature phrase to describe financial corruption. And, though complex in its twists and turns, the Enron story is fairly simple: crimes and lies motivated by greed. When Kenneth Lay was indicted in July 2004 for securities and wire fraud, it was really the endgame to a tawdry tale that exemplified the tight relationship between business, politics and the media.

Enron once ranked as the seventh largest company in the country. However, in December 2001, the company filed for bankruptcy, with Lay and top officials having been exposed as crooks who inflated profits and hid debt to the tune of billions of dollars. While some of his defenders and a few analysts claimed that Lay and his accomplishes like Jeffrey Skilling were only guilty of building a complex energy-trading system that failed, Lay's pathological behavior argues for a far more venal motive: he deliberately screwed his workers—publicly claiming that all was well with Enron, that the company did not face a liquidity crisis, while at the same time, just months before the company went belly-up, he was unloading almost a million Enron shares to cover his financial fortunes, cashing in $34 million. That wasn't all—as the company imploded in 2001, Lay was paid $104 million in salary bonuses and loans.[29]

For several years, Enron had been the darling of the business press, which wrote glowing articles about the energy giant that was conquering the world; with one or two exceptions, virtually no one questioned Enron's murky accounting practices. One of the few somewhat skeptical articles appeared on March 5, 2001, when reporter Bethany McLean wrote in *Fortune* that Enron, like a Hollywood movie star, was the "it" stock at the time: "While tech stocks were bombing at the box office last year, fans couldn't get enough of Enron, whose shares returned 89%. By almost every measure, the company turned in a virtuoso performance: Earnings increased 25%, and revenues more than doubled, to over $100 billion. Not surprisingly, the critics are gushing." Sounding a slightly ominous note, however, McLean went on to write about the wall that the company had built to shield its finances from outside eyes. "But for all the attention that's lavished on Enron, the company remains largely impenetrable to outsiders, as even some of its admirers are quick to admit. Start with a pretty straightforward question: How exactly does Enron make its money? Details are hard to come by because Enron keeps many of the specifics confidential for what it terms 'competitive reasons.'" Even those on Wall Street who scrutinized the company for a living were hard pressed to explain how it earned such incredible profits. "'If you figure it out, let me know,' laughed credit analyst Todd Shipman at Standard & Poor's. 'Do you have a year?' asked Ralph Pellecchia, Fitch's credit analyst, in response to the same question."[30]

It is important to note that McLean at no point suggested any nefarious dealings inside Enron, only that something didn't quite add up in the company's business model. This is a perfect example of how difficult it is for the media, the financial media in particular, whose livelihood depends on access to top business leaders, to question the motives or behavior of said leaders. Of such passivity, gullibility and pure boosterism are calamitous bubbles born.

In the political world, money from Enron washed all over state and federal officials, rewarding mostly Republicans but a fair number of Democrats as well. According to one report published by Public Citizen soon after the company went bankrupt, "Since 1989, 259 current members of Congress have received Enron campaign cash. This includes 188 Representatives (117 Republicans, 71 Democrats) and 71 Senators (41 Republicans, 29 Democrats)...Top current senators receiving Enron contributions since 1989: Kay Bailey Hutchison (R-Texas.), $99,500; Phil Gramm (R-Texas), $97,350; Conrad Burns (R-Montana), $23,200; and Charles Schumer (D-New York), $21,933 (Source: Center for Responsive Politics)...Top current representatives receiving Enron contributions since 1989: Ken Bentsen (D-Texas), $42,750; Sheila Jackson Lee (D-Texas), $38,000; Joe Barton (R-Texas), $28,909; Tom DeLay (R-Texas),

$28,900; and Martin Frost (D-Texas), $24,250 (Source: Center for Responsive Politics)."[31]

Another investigation by the Center for Public Integrity uncovered the intricate ties between the bipartisan elite world of money and law, showing how Enron bought the services of leading law firms, including Akin, Gump, Straus, Hauer & Feld; Bond Donatelli; Bracewell and Patterson; Davis Wright Tremaine; Price Waterhouse Coopers; Sideview Partners; Skadden Arps Meagher and Flom; Verner Liipfert Bernhard McPherson and Hand; Vinson & Elkins; and Quinn Gillespie—representing the full spectrum of Democratic and Republican dealmakers.[32] The same inquiry found that both political parties made deals with Enron that were suspiciously linked to campaign contributions: "During a trade trip to Bosnia and Croatia in July 1996, [Clinton Secretary of Commerce Ron] Brown's successor, Mickey Kantor, helped a senior Enron official that accompanied the secretary clinch a deal to construct a $100 million power plant, the *Boston Globe* reported. Six days before the trip began, Enron made a $100,000 contribution to the Democratic National Committee."

When Lay and Skilling were finally convicted, their victims, though financially devastated, felt a measure of vindication. "The sentence may not be to everyone's liking," said Debra Johnson, a former worker in the Enron International office. "But the verdict is about being fair to everyday working people…Skilling and Lay thought the money, the power was everything…This will let executives at other corporations know that it can happen to them. This is a milestone. And it's well deserved. We waited long enough. I'm smiling as I talk to you. I wish I'd been able to be there." Added Deborah Perrotta, a former administrative assistant: "Fantastic! Fantastic! …. It's a victory to show that corporate America can't get away with misleading the public and employees for their own personal gain."[33]

Despite the hopes of Ms. Perrotta, however, the corporate elite has, for the most part, yet to learn the lesson that crime doesn't pay. As a matter of fact, even after being caught, tried and convicted, many CEOs continued to proclaim their innocence:

Ken Lay: "I continue to grieve, as does my family, over the loss of the company and my failure to be able to save it...But failure does not equate to a crime."[34]

Bernard Ebbers: "It was only after the company was in desperate financial straits that I became involved...It was strictly a matter of survival."[35]

Dennis Kozlowski: "I did not oversee this in the manner in which I should have overseen that apartment...I'm here so I can explain to them why I'm innocent of all the charges against me."[36]

5. The Retirement Jackpot

I had no idea how talented Edward Whitacre was during his career at AT&T. Apparently, and you have to read between the lines to understand this, Whitacre did virtually everything at the company—he answered all the phones, went out to fix the underground cables, cleaned the bathrooms and was also, in his spare time, the CEO of the company.

How do we know that Whitacre did all this? Because, upon his retirement as CEO of AT&T in 2007, he received quite the pension package—far more than thousands of other AT&T workers—combined—would ever see. In addition to a $158 million payout and as much as $106 million in performance-based shares of the company, Whitacre also received automobile benefits, estimated at $24,000 per year; access to AT&T's corporate jet, at an estimated monthly cost of $20,000; home security ($6,500 annually); lifetime health and welfare benefits for him and his wife; and payment of taxes on all these benefits, at an estimated cost of $19,000 per year.[1] And if that retirement package—the third highest in U.S. corporate history—wasn't enough, Whitecare was also slated to receive $1 million annually for the three years following his retirement for acting as a "consultant" to AT&T.

The question that popped into my head when I read about Whitacre's retirement bounty was: Why should a man who has already earned millions of dollars in pay and benefits while he was working at a company receive millions of dollars more upon his retirement? As Paul Hodgson, senior research associate at the Corporate Library, an independent source for corporate governance and executive and director compensation information and analysis, pointed out about Whitacre, "They've been paying him salary, bonuses and long-term incentives for the 43 years he's been there…What is his pension for? As far as I know, the pension is to give you some financial security when you're finished working. It's not an incentive. I don't even think it [the pension] should be there, to be honest. Not at that level."[2]

Whitacre is far from an isolated case when it comes to huge corporate retirement packages. According to The Corporate Library, some of the other "parting gifts" awaiting America's leading CEOs include:

- Kenneth D. Lewis, Bank of America—$83 million
- H. Edward Hanway, Cigna—$73.2 million
- William C. Weldon, Johnson & Johnson—$64.2 million
- Alexander M. Cutler, Eaton Corp.—$54.6 million
- Samuel J. Palmisano, IBM—$53.8 million
- Harold M. Messmer, Jr., Robert Half International—$53.1 million
- Nolan D. Archibald, Black & Decker—$52 million
- Daniel P. Amos, Aflac—$50.1 million

And these large retirement packages are not restricted to just a few top executives, as the median CEO pension compensation package today is worth $6.4 million.[3]

In our tale of audacious greed, the annual salaries of corporate CEOs are really only a small part of the story—it is the pensions and related deferred compensation that these CEOs receive which is truly staggering. Until recently, these obscene amounts were often difficult to uncover because corporate boards did such a good job at hiding the figures. In the last few years, however, we've been able to learn more about CEO retirement packages because the Securities and Exchange Commission has toughened some of its disclosure rules, requiring more transparency and truth in reporting. Perhaps the funniest part of the new rules—and a comment on how long companies had gotten away with corporate thievery, in part, because of poor SEC oversight—came in the Commission's 2006 press release announcing the new, stricter reporting standards: "The rules will require companies to prepare most of this information **using plain English** principles in organization, language and design."[4] [emphasis added]. Translated into plain English, the press release basically admitted that CEOs had been bamboozling shareholders, regulators and the public for years by hiding and/or obscuring financial details in their company's official filings.

How 6 Equals 22

A dominant theme in both political and media circles in recent years has been the supposed "crisis" facing private pensions in many industries. "New Rules Urged to Avert Looming Pension Crisis" screamed the title of a *New York Times* article in 2003 about a government campaign "to bring attention to corporate pension plans, which they say may be on a road to collapse."[5] "Pension crisis comes to head with vote today," declared the *USA Today* in 2004, in an article that began, "Thousands of U.S. corporations are in limbo as Congress battles over a bill for pension-plan relief, and an April 15 payment deadline looms."[6] Fast forward to 2009, and if anything, the cries of crisis have grown even more shrill, mainly because of the economic meltdown, and have resulted in some companies taking direct action against their workers. For example, in May, the *Minneapolis Star Tribune* filed suit against the Teamsters local that represents its drivers so that the paper could stop funding the driver's pension plan.[7]

Because of the constant screams of "crisis," it has almost become an article of faith in the public lore that "generous" pensions for hardworking, regular people are the cause of many of the financial binds that private corporations (and municipalities) find themselves in today. Unfortunately, many Americans have internalized this notion—aided by the relentless stories on TV and in the newspapers about the supposed cause of bankruptcies in the airline and automobile industries, as well as a host of other examples. But the truth is that it is the corporate elite who have in fact created this pension "crisis," because of their personal greed.

You might remember that the airline industry was close to collapse back in 2002. Shares of Delta Airlines, for example, fell more than fifty percent, and the company lost $1.3 billion. On top of that, Delta also cut thousands of jobs. The company would eventually file for bankruptcy and only emerge from Chapter 11 in May 2007.

During this time, however, things weren't too bad for the company's CEO, Leo Mullin. Sure, he had to take a cut in pay after shareholders found out that, in the midst of the airline's demise, he had pocketed $2.2 million in salary and bonuses and $4.7 million in additional stock benefits.[8] But that was small change compared to the bounty of riches, buried in the fine print of the company's SEC filings, awaiting Mullin in the form of a supplemental executive-retirement plan or SERP. Even though Mullin had worked for Delta for less than six years, the company's board of directors waved its magic wand and decreed that he would be credited for an additional *twenty-two* years of service—that is not a misprint—which would entitle him to a pension that would provide him with a nice, tidy $1 million a year income. And, unlike regular workers' pensions that are hammered hard in a corporate bankruptcy, Mullin's SERP pension—and the similar SERP pensions handed out to a majority of the top executives in the country—cannot be touched in bankruptcy proceedings.

As far as those regular workers—in November 2002, Delta, concerned about its weakened cash position, announced that it was "phasing out" its secure defined-benefit pension plan for 56,000 nonunion workers. Apparently, the company was concerned about the "unsustainable rate" of the costs for the workers' pension plan, so the accounting knife came out to chop away anything that could be pared back, in the process altering the defined-benefit plan to a "cash balance" plan, which, because it does not guarantee the specific defined benefit that typically is set based on a worker's later years of employment, can dramatically lower pensions for older workers. While Mullin would be living the life of comfort and ease as a millionaire based on his pension alone, a 50-year-old flight attendant who had endured the hard work of flying and walking the aisles of Delta planes for twenty real years—as opposed to the invented years of service for Mullin—would have to live on an annual pension as low as $15,000.[9]

Mullin's burden on Delta wasn't unique—nor was the company's move to eliminate regular pensions while preserving them for corporate executives. As *The Wall Street Journal* noted in 2006, "Even as many companies reduce, freeze or eliminate pensions for workers—complaining of the costs—their executives are building up ever-bigger pensions, causing the companies' financial obligations for them to balloon."[10]

The Legacy Costs of Greedy CEOs

A corollary to the media and political fixation on the pension "crisis" are stories about the long-term pension and healthcare benefit commitments that companies like General Motors have made to their employees. According to the prevailing logic, unless these so-called "legacy costs" are drastically reduced, companies like GM will never be profitable. As an example, in 2005, *Business Week* wrote that, "within five years GM must become a much smaller company, with fewer brands, fewer models, and reduced legacy costs."[11] While GM did owe $87.8 billion in pension benefits to its 700,000 U.S. workers and retirees in 2006, what was often overlooked by the media was that the company had set aside $95.3 billion to pay for those benefits, meaning that its pension obligations to its workers was in fact fully funded. (And that $95 billion also earned GM a pretty penny: $10 billion per year in investment income alone). However, during the same year, the pension plan for General Motor's executives was *underfunded* by $1.4 billion.[12] Thus, it was not the legacy costs owed to regular workers that were hurting GM's bottom line, but the pensions paid out to the company's executives.

GM is not the only company that pays pensions to its executives with money it doesn't actually have. Boosted by surging pay and rich formulas, General Electric experienced a $3.5 billion liability in executive pensions in 2006; AT&T, $1.8 billion; Exxon Mobil and IBM approximately $1.3 billion each; Bank of America and Pfizer about $1.1 billion apiece.[13] Overall, benefits for executives now account for a significant share of pension obligations in the United States.; at some companies, obligations for a single executive's pension may approach $100 million. As a result, the money companies save by curtailing pensions for regular retirees—totaling billions of dollars in recent years—is often used to mask the rising cost of benefits for executives. While pension obligations to regular workers are stable or shrinking at many companies, those for executives are on the rise. At BellSouth, for example, the obligations for pensions for ordinary workers edged down 3 percent from 2000 to 2006, while the liability for pensions for executives went up 89 percent.[14]

Things have gotten so out of whack that at some companies, the debt owed to executives is higher than the pension money **owed to the rest of the company's workforce**. As *The Wall Street Journal* observed: "Even as companies have complained about the cost of retiree benefits, they have been awarding larger pay and pensions to executives. At Goldman, for example, the $11.8 billion obligation primarily for deferred executive compensation dwarfed the liability for its broad-based pension plan for all employees. That was just $399 million, and fully funded with set-aside assets....Bank of America Corp.'s $1.3 billion liability for supplemental executive pensions reduced earnings by $104 million in 2007, filings show. By contrast, the bank's regular pension plan is overfunded, and the surplus helped the plan contribute $32 million to earnings last year."[15] The pension money owed by Goldman Sachs to its executives is 33 times the amount the company owes to the rest of its workers—and the average workers' pension plan has all its assets.

In addition, as the pace of greed has quickened, emboldened CEOs are no longer content with the big hauls they are already getting, but are also looking for new ways to make those mountains of cash grow even taller, as *Wall Street Journal* reporter Mark Maremont uncovered in early 2009:

> Some major companies are boosting the value of retirement plans for top executives by using a generous formula when converting a pension into a single lump-sum payment. The practice, which remained largely unknown until a recent change in federal disclosure requirements, can increase the value of a CEO's pension by 10% to 40%, sometimes amounting to millions of extra dollars. The additional sums aren't always fully reflected in annual pension-benefit tables included in proxy statements, or in company financial statements, due to the complexities of accounting and disclosure rules.[16]

The way this works is simple: a CEO receives the payout of his pension benefits in one lump sum, at a very favorable interest rate. It's a nice scam, as Ramani Ayer, the 61-year-old chairman and CEO of Hartford Financial Services Group certainly is aware: when he retires, he'll walk away with a pension of $37 million, versus what he actually has accumulated based on his service at the company ($27 million) because he'll take the money in a lump sum, as opposed to having it paid out every year. The same is true of John Hammergren, the CEO of McKesson Corp., a drug wholesaler, as the company will ladle $11 million more into his lump sum pension, raising his overall take to $85 million.[17]

Of course, most regular workers don't have the luxury of having their pensions paid out in one lump sum payment, under favorable terms. Quite the opposite: while CEOs have been busy bulking up their pension benefits, tens of millions of Americans, who have put small amounts of money in their 401(k) retirement accounts every year to save for a stable retirement, have been opening up their statements and seeing steep declines in their savings because of the 2008 financial crisis and simultaneous nosedive in the stock market.

An even more insidious corporate greed scam was exposed by the *Wall Street Journal* in May of 2009. According to the *Journal*, "Banks are using a little-known tactic to help pay bonuses, deferred pay and pensions they owe executives. They're holding life-insurance policies on hundreds of thousands of their workers, with themselves as the beneficiaries."[18] Apparently, the banks took out the majority of these policies during the mortgage bubble, when executive pay was on the increase, and banking regulators "affirmed the use of life insurance as a way to finance executive pay and benefits." As of the end of 2008, banks held a total of $122.3 billion worth of life insurance on their employees, nearly double the $65.8 billion they held at the end of 2004. Bank of America was top on the list, holding $17.3 billion worth of life insurance on its employees, with Wachovia following at $12 billion, J.P. Morgan Chase at $11.1 billion and Wells Fargo at $5.7 billion. In the case of J.P. Morgan, while the company had $10 billion in deferred-pay obligations at the end of 2008, these obligations were more than offset by $12 billion in bank-owned employee life insurance.

Not surprisingly, this practice hurts regular employees and their families. In many cases, as an incentive to get them to name the company as their beneficiary, employees are offered a small portion of their death benefits. However, this coverage usually ends when the employee separates from the company. In December 2008, Irma Johnson mistakenly received a check from the Security Life of Denver Insurance Co. for $1.6 million, payable to Amegy Bank, which had employed her husband, Daniel. According to a lawsuit filed by Mrs. Johnson, "the bank told her husband, Daniel Johnson, a credit risk manager who had survived two brain surgeries, that he was eligible for supplemental life insurance of $150,000, if he signed a consent form authorizing the bank to purchase an insurance policy on his life. Four months later, the bank fired him." Mr. Johnson died from a brain tumor in 2008, at the age of forty-one. His wife and children? They received no life insurance benefits, because the bank had canceled them when Mr. Johnson was fired.[19]

$5,270 vs. $1.92

Another way that the CEOs of America are enriching their retirements is by using employee pension money to fund their own pensions. While companies have been freezing or cutting back employee pensions over the past several years, they have simultaneously been converting the accumulated assets into cash to underwrite executive retirement benefits. Another piece in *The Wall Street Journal* tells us all about the practice:

> In recent years, companies from Intel Corp. to CenturyTel Inc. collectively have moved hundreds of millions of dollars of obligations for executive benefits into rank-and-file pension plans. This lets companies capture tax breaks intended for pensions of regular workers and use them to pay for executives' supplemental benefits and compensation. The practice has drawn scant notice. A close examination by *The Wall Street Journal* shows how it works and reveals that the maneuver, besides being a dubious use of tax law, risks harming regular workers. It can drain assets from pension plans and make them more likely to fail. Now, with the current bear market in stocks weakening many pension plans, this practice could put more in jeopardy.[20]

The scheme itself is a bit convoluted. Normally, pension plans treat both regular and highly-compensated employees in the same manner. Therefore, to funnel more cash to their corporate higher-ups, companies offer what are known as "supplemental" executive pension plans. Here's the rub: companies can't deduct the costs of these supplemental plans. Because of this, companies are always looking for a way to fleece workers and taxpayers (because contributions to pension plans are tax-deductible). After years of trying, they finally found a way, as the example of Intel, the computer chipmaker, shows. Back in 2005, the company moved more than $200 million of its deferred-comp IOUs into its pension plan. The company then added $187 million in cash to the plan. The result: when the company's executives collected their deferred salaries, Intel didn't have to pay them out of the company's coffers, as the pension plan paid them instead. And since companies can only deduct the cost of deferred compensation when they actually pay it out—which is often years in the future—Intel's contribution to their pension plan was immediately deductible, saving the company $65 million in 2005. Ultimately, the majority of the assets in Intel's pension plan that the company can deduct as an expense ended up in the pockets of the company's highest-earners, a grand total of 4 percent of Intel's workforce.[21]

However, companies have to be careful when they try to run this sham, as the IRS requires that pension plans not discriminate between lower-paid and higher-paid workers. So what have the corporate pension consultants conjured up to get around this requirement? Simple: give large benefits to the highly-paid workers, and tiny increases to regular workers. For example, Royal & SunAlliance, an insurance company, laid off 228 employees when it sold one of its divisions in 1999. Right before the sale, however, the company amended the division's pension plan, awarding larger benefits to several departing officers and directors (one human resources executive received an additional $5,270 a month for life). To make this scam kosher in the eyes of the IRS, the company had to give minute pension increases to 100 lower paid workers. One worker "got an increase of $1.92 a month." Joseph Gromala, a middle manager who stood to get $8.87 more a month when he turned sixty-five, "wrote to the company seeking details about higher sums other people were receiving. A lawyer wrote back saying the company didn't have to show him the relevant pension-plan amendment."[22]

"Everything Is Just Heading South"

In our era of audacious greed, the better things get for the corporate elite, the worse they get for the American worker. Consider that:

- Only 21 percent of private sector workers have a defined benefit pension plan, and 29 percent have only a defined contribution plan. Fifty percent have nothing.[23]
- At the end of 2007, the average 401(k) account balance was $65,454, while the median account balance was $18,942.[24] And even those numbers are deceptive, as the average was pulled up because the top ten percent of income earners have the ability to put an extra $10,000 to $15,000 into their accounts at the end of the year. In addition, those numbers don't even reflect the devastation of the 2008 financial crisis.
- If current trends continue, we are heading into a period where income for retired Americans will fall for the first time since the Great Depression.

The truth is that while the Leo Mullins of the world are living large off their extravagant pensions, most Americans are like Dick Boice. Employed for thirty years by IBM, Boice was planning to retire and relocate to Arizona with his wife Lauren. However, when the planned date for his retirement came, Boise was still on the job at IBM, and intended to be with the company for several more years. The reason: the Boices had hoped to sell their home to boost their retirement income but because of the housing downturn, were unable to do so. At the same time, the value of Dick Boice's 401(k) and individual retirement accounts was falling by 20 percent. "Everything is just heading south," said Mr. Boice. "You can't hardly make any kinds of plans because you don't know what you can count on."[25]

Perhaps more than any single piece of the story, the pension debacle best exposes the phony promise of the "free market." On the one hand, you have the regular citizens of this country, people like

Dick Boice, who in less than two years have lost close to $2 trillion of the money they invested in their pensions and 401(k) plans.[26] Unlike defined-benefit plans, people could reach into their 401(k) plans and take money out, which they have done with alarming regularity over the past few years—not to purchase fur coats and yachts but to simply pay bills they could no longer afford with maxed out credit cards and home equity loans that no longer existed when housing values plummeted. "Everyone wiped their hands of any obligation for retirement, and the burden shifted from the employer to the employee, and the risk is shifted from the employer to the employee," said Representative George Miller (D-California), chairman of the House Committee on Education and Labor who has been one of the sharpest critics of the ideology of the free market. "In the beginning, no one ever said, 'Would this be sufficient? Would it work?' and what you see is a plan that is highly responsive to external events unlike Social Security, unlike defined-benefit plans, unlike a public pension plan."[27]

Of course, the elites who shoved 401(k) plans down the throats of the public just shrugged and effectively said, well, that's life in the "free market." "If you own equities, you really have to believe in the American capitalist system in that the dollars will find the highest and best use," said Mickey Cargile, a managing partner for WNB Private Client Services, a financial advisory firm in Texas. "Along with that, there will be a period in which the excesses in the market will be purged. That's what we're seeing now. That's what we saw in 1987."[28]

Well, not exactly. While the "excesses" in the market—the end result of the behavior of the financial elite that led to the economic crisis in 2008—were being "purged," the pensions of these same elites were unaffected—and often increased—because their benefits had been enhanced by a series of "creative" maneuvers that protected against anything that happened in the "free market." However, these creative safeguards didn't protect the savings of regular people. "The recent unstable financial crisis is having a devastating effect on my life," recalled Roberta Quan, a retired school teacher from San Pablo, California, who is caring for her husband, who has Alzheimer's. "A lifetime of savings in catastrophic decline is demoralizing. The bottom line is that I am retired and unable to re-earn lost funds."[29] Similarly, Steve Carroll, a retired writer from Petaluma, California, said, "Our monthly budget has been severely depleted for life. We still have our IRAs. But, as they are in mutual stock funds they are so far down in value that selling any of them right now, as the law requires of [my partner] Chuck, the loss would be an enormous percentage of the investment."[30]

In the end, the rhetoric of the "free market" allowed a small elite to rob the treasuries of companies to pad their own already lavish retirements. The only silver lining in the whole pension debacle—and, unfortunately, one that provides little solace to people who have lost their homes or are trying to cope with an austere retirement—is that we now have a bracing reminder of the failure of the so-called "free market" and, conversely, the need for a publicly-backed, solid pension system that goes hand in hand with Social Security.

6. How to Screw Up Your Company—And Still Get Rich

I am making the following offer to all corporate boards in the United States: I am available to run your company, no matter what industry you are in, despite the fact that, in most cases, I have zero knowledge about that industry, or even your particular company. As a result of my ignorance, it is more than likely that, under my leadership, your company's stock price will fall, its profits will decline and it will lose market share. Therefore, the chances are good that within a year, two at the most, you will have to fire me.

I will do all this for $250,000 a year in salary, and the same healthcare and pension benefits that you give to your regular workers. In addition, when you fire me, I will leave with just three months' severance pay, and no additional perks—no golf club memberships, no use of the company's corporate jet. Though my tenure will wind up costing your company millions of dollars, in the end, you will still be getting a much better deal than many companies have gotten over the past decade.

If I'm lucky, my stint as CEO of Any Company USA might qualify me for the McKinnell Award, which is given out annually by the Investors for Director Accountability.[1] The award was established in 2007 in recognition of Henry McKinnell's performance as CEO of Pfizer. To this day, McKinnell's tenure is hard to forget, in particular if you are a Pfizer shareholder. In 2001, when McKinnell took over as CEO, Pfizer's stock was trading at about $45 a share;

when his tenure ended five years later, Pfizer's stock was floundering at under $36 a share. On McKinnell's watch, the value of the company declined by $137 billion.

However, McKinnell did not suffer for his reign of error at Pfizer. On the contrary; as he walked out the door at the end of 2006, having presided over a loss of 40 percent in the value of the company, McKinnell still had quite a wad of cash to stuff in his pocket: $12 million in severance pay; a bonus of $2.15 million; and a hunk of stocks that had vested, worth $5.8 million. In addition, he also received a $78 million payout for deferred compensation, along with about $18.3 million in "performance-based shares."[2] And as if that wasn't enough, McKinnell will be cashing an annual pension check of $6.65 million—for the rest of his life.

The case of Henry McKinnell demonstrates that, despite what they may teach aspiring young executives in business school, top performance is not the key to financial success. Instead, even if your company posts poor results and you lose the confidence of your shareholders, as a CEO, you can still pocket millions of dollars. Basically, in the world of CEO greed, its high pay all the way, no matter the actual results you generate.

Zero Value Created, Millions of Dollars Paid

Robert Nardelli is another example of the curious phenomena of tying CEO pay to non-performance. Nardelli joined General Electric in 1971 as a manufacturing engineer, rising to Senior Vice President in 1995. While he ultimately lost out in the competition to succeed Jack Welch as CEO of GE, Nardelli still received a lucrative consolation prize: an extravagant offer from venture capitalist Ken Langone (who sat on the boards of both GE and Home Depot) to run Home Depot, even though Nardelli had no prior retail experience.

During his six-year stint as CEO of Home Depot, Nardelli created absolutely no value for the company's shareholders. I am not exaggerating: on December 4, 2000, the day before Nardelli was named chief executive, shares of Home Depot closed at $40.75; on

December 29, 2006, the last day of trading before he announced his resignation as CEO, the stock closed at $40.16.[3] For lowering Home Depot's stock price by 59 cents over the course of six years, Nardelli received "$210 million in cash and stock options, including a $20 million severance payment and retirement benefits of $32 million," upon his separation from the company.[4] This was in addition to the "$125.57 million in annual salary, bonuses, stocks and other payments" he earned during his entire tenure at Home Depot (In 2006 alone, Nardelli pulled down $38.1 million in compensation).[5] Long known for an abrasive and confrontational management style, Nardelli was ultimately forced out as CEO when Home Depot's board of directors revolted when he refused to accept even a symbolic reduction in his stock package—though he agreed to give up a guarantee that he wouldn't necessarily receive a minimum $3 million bonus each year, he refused to tie his future stock awards to shareholder gains.[6] This apparently angered some of the company's board members—though, to be clear, this was the same board that had initially approved Nardelli's extraordinary compensation. About the board of directors' complicity, nationally known compensation analyst and activist Nell Minow said, "They overpaid him when he arrived. They overpaid him while he was there. And they overpaid him on the way out the door. They've handled this horribly from beginning to end."[7]

No wonder Nardelli was so magnanimous in late 2008 when he publicly offered to take just one dollar in annual salary in return for landing taxpayer dollars to bailout Chrysler, the company he had been hired in 2007 to run by Cerberus Capital Management, the private equity firm that bought the auto company. It's not hard to be generous when you are living off the income generated by a previous nine-figure haul, a haul you earned by helping your company lose money.

Alpha CEOs

The roster of CEOs who have ruined their companies yet still reaped large financial rewards is huge, and spread across every sector throughout the economy. While it's hard to choose from the many examples, let's take a look at a few of the most egregious ones.

Frank Newman was a former Deputy Treasury Secretary who in 1995 traded in his fairly pedestrian government salary for a massive compensation package to head up Bankers Trust—a company that was still reeling from a financial scandal involving derivatives gone south. By the fall of 1998, the company's stock had gone from $136 per share to $59, a financial wipeout that extinguished almost $8 billion in value. Yet what was Newman doing that September, just after announcing a huge trading loss? What any responsible CEO would be doing: jumping on the company's corporate jet and flying to Paris with his wife for a long weekend. "I thought we were going to be working all weekend," one banker told Fortune, which reported that Newman and his wife made such frequent use of the jet that the flight personnel dubbed them "Alpha" and "Alpha2." [8] The couple also went decidedly upscale when it came to their housing choices, moving from a shack worth just $3 million to a much more appropriate set of digs for people of their stature: a $9.8 million pad on Fifth Avenue. "He used to be a conservative guy when I knew him in San Francisco [where Newman worked at BankAmerica]," recalled a banker at another firm. "Now he's traded in his Ford Fairlane for a corporate jet."[9]

In November 1998, with the company's stock price in the cellar, Newman agreed to sell Bankers Trust to Deutsche Bank for $9.8 billion; by June 1999, Newman had been shoved out of the merged operation. But, don't shed any tears for the guy. Even though he mismanaged the company during his stint as CEO, he was still able to walk away with pay and benefits estimated at between $50 and $100 million.[10]

Pharmacy delivery giant Caremark's 2006 merger with drugstore chain CVS triggered a golden parachute for Caremark CEO Edwin Crawford—roughly $287 million, not including health and other benefits that he will receive for the remaining eight years of his employment agreement. But there was some doubt as to whether the merger was actually good for Caremark's shareholders; a public pension fund in Louisiana sued the directors of the company, contending that "their unanimous backing of the company's $21 billion merger with CVS over a rival $26 billion bid from Express Scripts improperly benefits Caremark executives at the expense of shareholders."[11] In addition, several executives were paid a total of $103 million in severance, even though they in fact stayed at the company once it merged with CVS.[12]

When it comes to impressive compensation for unimpressive performance, however, look no further than Michael Ovitz. After just one year on the job, the former super agent was fired as the president of Disney by the man who had hand-picked him for the position, Michael Eisner. Ovitz's exit package for a year of failure: $109 million in cash and stock severance. During a subsequent shareholder lawsuit, it was revealed that Ovitz managed to spend $6 million of the company's cash, including $2 million to remodel his office and almost $100,000 for choice courtside seats at Los Angeles Lakers' basketball games.[13]

Then there is Charles Prince of Citigroup. In his four years as CEO, Prince oversaw a financial return that averaged a negative 2.5 percent per year. Yes, that's right, a negative return—compared to a 12 percent a year return for the Standard & Poor's 500 index during the same time period.[14] When he resigned from his job in November 2007, after a nearly $6 billion write-down because of mortgage securities' risks, Prince said, "Given the size of the recent losses in our mortgage-backed securities business, the only honorable course for me to take as Chief Executive Officer is to step down."

Apparently, Prince's "honor" did not prevent him from accepting a $10.4 million discretionary bonus, which the board of Citigroup could have said no to, but didn't. The board also let Prince keep more than $28 million in unvested stock and options. In addition, Prince also walked away with pensions and retirement benefits worth $1.8 million. All this for generating a negative financial return for Citigroup's stockholders during his run as CEO.

Bankruptcy—The Failure that Keeps Giving

To most people, the word "bankruptcy" equates to financial failure. Therefore, you would think that when a corporation declares bankruptcy, it would mean a dismal financial outlook for the company, a tightening of the financial belt, along with smaller paychecks for both management and workers. You would be right about all that—except when it comes to today's greedy corporate CEOs.

Take Robert S. Miller, a takeover artist who specializes in gaining control over struggling companies, jettisoning their pension plans into the hands of the federal government and then selling off the company for a large profit. When he was CEO of Bethlehem Steel in 2002, Miller shut down the company's pension plan, shoveling $3.7 billion in unfunded obligations for retirees onto the federal government. He then teamed with Wilbur L. Ross, another leveraged buyout king, and together they combined Bethlehem with four other ailing steel companies and sold the combined concern for $4.5 billion—money which was not turned over to help the workers of the respective companies but instead pocketed by Ross, Miller and other high-flying vultures who profit in the area known as "distressed assets."

Miller's greed reached its most audacious level, however, when he took over as CEO at Delphi Corporation, an auto parts supplier, and led the company into bankruptcy. As part of his plan to emerge from bankruptcy, Miller demanded that workers at Delphi agree to cut their pay more than half, from approximately $26 an hour to $12.50 an hour. He also asked for the right to dump the company's pension obligations on the government, essentially promising workers that, in exchange for giving up money in their paychecks today, the company would make sure they had a decent retirement.

And what was the sacrifice that Miller proposed for himself and his fellow executives in order to save Delphi? Under the company's proposed employee-compensation plan, Delphi would allocate $21.8 million for cash bonuses to executives during the first six months of bankruptcy, plus an additional $87.9 million for 486 U.S. executives who would receive between 30 percent and 250 percent of their salaries once Delphi emerged from bankruptcy. There would also be a severance package under which Delphi's top 21 officers would collect up to 18 months' salary and target bonuses, 89 other executives would get a year's salary and bonuses, and 373 others would receive a year's pay. Finally, the top 600 worldwide executives with Delphi would receive 10 percent of the equity in the reorganized company, a stake worth $400 million.[15] Interesting definition of sacrifice, wouldn't you say?

Unsurprisingly, Miller's plan didn't sit well with either the United Auto Workers or the Pension Benefit Guaranty Corporation, a federal corporation which protects the pensions of more than 44 million current and retired workers. The PBGC filed a motion against the proposals of Miller and his cronies, saying that their plan wasn't "a sound business decision" that would aid in Delphi's recovery. The PBGC was concerned that "hundreds of millions of dollars would go to executives at a time when Delphi may not be able to pay $400 million due its pension plan" the following January."[16]

Miller himself offered a unique window into the mentality of the elite class that has engineered the corporate plundering of America. When asked in 2002 about the arrest of John Rigas, who would go to jail for siphoning a fortune out of Adelphi Communications, Miller said, "I'm quite happy that the government has acted against the few C.E.O.'s who have caused such reputational damage to business. It proves that C.E.O.'s can't just hire more lawyers and get away with crimes."[17] But, when asked about the obscene financial arrangements he orchestrated at Delphi, Miller was quoted in several interviews as saying that the compensation program was necessary to keep top executives from leaving the company during the bankruptcy process, and that hourly workers were overpaid at Delphi while the company's top managers and executives were underpaid. In Miller's moral framework, buttressed by the perverted values of the "free market," he could clearly see the damage wrought by the Rigas' of the world, but had no grasp—or at least, feigned to have no grasp—of the damage his own actions inflicted on the workers under him at Delphi. Ultimately, the UAW was able to convince the bankruptcy court to force a sharp reduction in the incentive pay that Miller wanted to shovel out to his fellow executives.[18]

The Bull is Gored

No group better exemplifies the "failure can make you rich" scheme than the dealmakers on Wall Street. Contrary to what they were telling the media during the 2008 financial crisis, the big shots on "The Street" were not the innocent victims of a once in a lifetime financial crisis that nobody could have foreseen. In truth, they were not victims at all, but rather orchestrators of a worldwide economic meltdown that was the direct result of gross mismanagement driven by greed. Basically, the goal of the high flyers on Wall Street was not the health of their companies or the health of the American economy, but instead a single-minded desire to drive earnings and stock prices as high as possible so that they could continue to demand ever higher compensation and collect ever greater power.

For an example, let's start with one of America's most well-known firms, Merrill Lynch. Once an iconic symbol and standard bearer of Wall Street, in 2008 alone, the company lost $27 billion, $15 billion of it in the fourth quarter of the year—a massive implosion that had been forecast when the company agreed that September to sell itself to Bank of America, a sale that came about not as a strategic combination often referred to, in the business parlance, as the "synergy" of two compatible companies, but in a desperate attempt to avoid the fate of Lehman Brothers which, on the very same day that Merrill's fate was sealed, announced it was filing for bankruptcy and headed for liquidation.[19]

Thanks to the financial collapse of Merrill Lynch, thousands of people lost their jobs—mainly secretaries, administrative assistants, clerks and a whole host of other regular workers who only knew what a multi-million dollar bonus was by reading about it in the newspaper. The fate of the company's management? E. Stanley O'Neal, who, as chairman and CEO from 2003 to 2007 was at the helm of the company when Merrill posted a $2.24 billion loss in the third-quarter of 2007 because of a mind-boggling $8.4 billion write-down on investments in junk mortgages and risky debt securities—the largest quarterly loss in the company's nearly 100-year history—walked away with a "retirement" compensation package worth $161 million. (And what was O'Neal doing while his company was suffering record losses? Playing golf—including three rounds on three different courses in a single day.)[20]

O'Neal's successor, John Thain, was just as good at the pay for failure game, pocketing $83.1 million in compensation in 2007 so that he could oversee that spectacular 2008 fourth-quarter $15 billion loss, which forced Merrill's new owners, Bank of America, to go hat in hand to the federal government asking for billions of dollars in taxpayer bailout money on top of $25 billion they had already received.[21] (Because of his exceptional work as CEO, Thain asked for an additional $10 million bonus at the end of 2008, which, in a rare case of corporate governance backbone, was denied by Merrill's board.[22]) Thain's service to Merrill was further distinguished by his spending $1 million of the company's funds to redecorate his office, which included buying a $1,405 trash can.[23]

Thain wasn't the only executive at Merrill Lynch who succeeded by failing. Peter Kraus, who was hired at the time of the sale of the company to Bank of America, quit the day the sale was completed. His bonus for just three months work—a tidy $24.9 million, which works out to roughly about $249,000 a day. And, lest you think that Kraus was distraught about leaving Merrill Lynch, on the very day he left the company, he and his wife closed on a $36 million luxury co-op on Park Ave.[24]

Mirror, mirror on the wall...

Here's a question to ponder: does Stephen Schwarzman still stare at the giant portrait of himself that hangs in his living room and think about what a financial genius he is—even though his company, the private equity firm Blackstone, lost $232 million in the first quarter of 2009?[25] I'm going to bet that a man who has the desperate need to constantly look at a larger than life representation of himself is not capable of admitting that the vision he has of himself as a financial wunderkind is, based on real world results, a fantasy.

As the individual with the largest single stake in the Blackstone Group, Schwarzman scored a very lucrative payday when the firm went public in 2007:

- He received $684 million from the proceeds of the company's initial public offering and its equity sale to an affiliate of the Chinese government.[26]

- Schwarzman also received 233,987,965 Blackstone units, worth $7.25 billion at the time of the IPO.[27] The offering price at the time was $31 per share.[28] However, eighteen months after the IPO, with Blackstone's share price below $6, the value of Schwarzman's equity in the firm was down more than 80 percent.[29]

- Schwarzman received equity in Blackstone subsidiaries valued by the company at $728,798,713. This too is likely to be worth far less today than it was in 2007 due to the company's poor performance over the past two years.

- On top of the windfall he received from Blackstone's IPO, Schwarzman also earned $350.2 million in cash distributions in 2007 as a result of his profits interest in the private equity and hedge funds Blackstone managed.[30] In addition, he was paid a base salary of $175,000 and received several perquisites, including a personal car with driver and use of a private plane, valued at $179,482.[31]

On top of earning a lot of money, Schwarzman also seems to have a compulsive need to flaunt his wealth, as he has engaged in some ostentatious spending sprees over the years. His sixtieth birthday party in 2007 is already the stuff of society legend in over-the-top self-indulgence. Held in New York City's cavernous Park Armory, whose entrance was redone to resemble the birthday boy's apartment, the event included performances by Patti LaBelle, who sang a song about Schwarzman, and Rod Stewart. The emcee was comedian Martin Short. The tab for the party: $3 million. And, to top things off, the massive portrait of Schwarzman was temporarily borrowed from his living room and hung in the Armory for all to gaze upon.[32]

The birthday party was just the tip of the iceberg when it came to Schwarzman's spending orgy. As detailed in *The New Yorker*, "In May, 2000, Schwarzman paid $37 million—reportedly a record sum at the time for a Manhattan co-op—for a thirty-five-room triplex on Park Avenue that was once owned by John D. Rockefeller, Jr. In 2003, he paid $20.5 million for Four Winds, the former E. F. Hutton estate in Florida, which occupies a choice spit of land between the ocean and the Intracoastal waterway....In 2006, he paid $34 million for a Federal-style house, on eight acres on Mecox Bay, in the Hamptons, that was previously owned by the Vanderbilt heir Carter Burden." In addition to those homes, Schwarzman also owns a coastal estate in Saint-Tropez and a beachfront property in Jamaica. The total value of the five properties: $125 million. "I love houses," Schwarzman told *The New Yorker*. "I'm not sure why."[33]

Based on the grandiose and very public expressions of his wealth, you would at least think that the actual financial performance of the Blackstone Group under Schwarzman's leadership would be strong. Guess again. In fact, many of the investments that the company has made under Schwarzman's watch have turned sour. For example, though Schwarzman got fabulously rich from Blackstone's IPO, the company actually began losing money immediately after it went public. In the first quarter after its IPO, the third quarter of 2007, the company suffered a $113 million net loss. During the same period a year later, the third quarter of 2008, Blackstone's net loss more than tripled to $340 million.[34] That was enough to spook investors; Blackstone was forced to liquidate two hedge funds in December 2008 because the company couldn't get enough people to entrust it with their money.

The list of the company's failures under Schwarzman doesn't end there. Beginning in 2006, Blackstone started investing in India, eventually spending approximately $730 million in the country. Among the projects was $150 million that the company put into a construction firm, Nagarjuna Construction. Unfortunately, Nagarjuna's shares have declined more than 70 percent since Blackstone's initial investment in August 2007. Blackstone also put $60 million into Allcargo Global Logistics, a transportation company, whose stock price dropped more than 50 percent within eight months of the investment.[35] Blackstone also tried to get into the Asian markets, opening an office in Hong Kong, but abruptly shut down the office only five months later. According to the company, its subsidiary GSO, intended to open an Asian debt trading desk, but after five months had not bought a single bond or loan.[36]

Blackstone's domestic track is no better. In October 2007, as the credit bubble was beginning to burst, the company completed a $26 billion leveraged buyout of the Hilton Hotel Corporation.[37] However, during the final quarter of 2008, performance in the hotel industry began to decline dramatically, with the average revenue per available room dropping 8.2 percent from September through the end of the year. (Given the state of the economy, the decline is expected to continue through at least 2009.) But in order to make the deal with Blackstone, Hilton had to take on more than $20 billion in debt, which will become increasingly difficult for the company to repay as profits continue to decline. Ultimately, this may threaten Hilton's solvency. Of course, Schwarzman and his gang don't care: they have already pocketed large fees from the deal.

Blackstone also managed $29 billion in investment funds dedicated to the real estate market, nearly $7.5 billion of which was invested at the peak of the real estate bubble in 2006 and 2007. Despite the dramatic decline in real estate prices over the past two years, Goldman Sachs reported in November 2008 that Blackstone was still recording the value of its total portfolio of real estate assets as if it was worth 20 percent more than the purchase price—an inflation of value that, of course, makes Blackstone—and thus Schwarzman—seem more profitable than they in fact are.[38]

The reason that Blackstone needs to inflate the value of its assets is because Schwarzman and other company employees have received more than $1.3 billion in performance bonuses, which are based on internal estimates of the value of investments that have yet to pay off. If Blackstone ultimately sells these investments for a lower price than they estimated when they paid out these bonuses—which was at the top of the market bubble—the investors in Blackstone's private equity, real estate and hedge funds will have to be reimbursed. Indeed, Blackstone currently owes investors in its private equity funds more than $107 million because it paid out bonuses to its employees based on the value of the investments at the height of the bubble; the investments that have since declined in value. (Investors in Blackstone's real estate funds are owed $25.4 million.) So there is a kind of shell game being played here that is fairly typical in the private equity world: pretend like something is worth a bunch of money now, pocket a bonus off of that inflated value, and then try to hide the actual loss down the road, since if you have to own up to the real value, you will have to then pay back the bonuses based on that value.

Finally, in between admiring the portrait of his grand self and jetting off to one of his opulent homes, Schwarzman also has a bit of a legal problem hanging over his head: He is one of the defendants in a class action suit brought by some unhappy Blackstone investors. The suit claims that Blackstone's prospectuses contained false and misleading information because the company failed to disclose that several of its portfolio companies were struggling financially.

Per the complaint, Blackstone is accused of failing "to disclose that certain of the Company's portfolio companies were not performing well and were of declining value as, as a result, Blackstone's equity investment was impaired and the company would not generate anticipated performance fees on those investments or would have fees 'clawed-back' by limited partners in its funds." [39] All of that is legalese for a cover-up.

In a November 2007 speech that echoed Michael Douglas's infamous "greed is good" speech from the movie *Wall Street*, Schwarzman told his audience that, "Private equity is here to stay as a significant force and as a force for good within much of the world economy." For those who didn't fully absorb his point, Schwarzman went on, "Let me repeat that: as *a force for good*." Of course, one would have to ask Schwarzman what his definition of "good" is: while Blackstone has certainly been good to him over the years—*Forbes* declared him the 145th richest person in the world in 2008, with an estimated worth of $6.5 billion (though he fell to 261st place on the list for 2009, with an estimated worth of only $2.5 billion)[40]—Blackstone lost $1.16 billion in 2008, and its stock price has fallen 88 percent since its initial public offering in June of 2007.[41] In the end, it would seem that what is "good" for Schwarzman is not necessarily good for Blackstone's investors.

Corporate Boards: A CEOs Best Friend

After reading these tales of CEOs who prospered while their companies tanked, you must be asking yourself: why? Why would corporations, whose primary goal is earning a profit, throw away their money on chief executive officers who presided over often staggering financial loses? While companies will often use vague, legal terms like "employment contract" when trying to excuse the outrageous salaries they pay their CEOs, to find the real culprit behind the reward for failure model, you need to look at the people who are actually responsible for the internal governance and oversight of these companies. I'm talking, of course, about the board of directors.

From the compliant board which allowed Robert Nardelli to get rich despite creating zero value for Home Depot, to the directors that let Charles Price keep a $10.4 million bonus at Citigroup despite generating a negative return for the company, lack of corporate governance—which is supposed to be the primary role of boards—has had the effect of rewarding many CEOs for failing. Unfortunately, instead of acting as independent entities like they are supposed to, many corporate boards are instead comprised of friends and cronies of the CEO, which essentially means that governance goes out the window, in favor of nepotism.

To use a hypothetical example, if a CEO—let's call him Stanley—running company X makes $10 million a year, you would think that his counterpart at another company—Harvey—in order to get $10 million for himself, would need to argue to his board that if he didn't get the same salary as Stanley, he wouldn't be a happy camper and might look elsewhere for employment. However, based on the way things are done today at many companies, instead of having to issue threats to the board, Harvey can just make sure that his friends (Tom, Dick and Harry) are on his board's compensation committee, which set the CEO's pay and stock options package. Tom, Dick and Harry will of course make certain that Harvey is always royally compensated, whether or not he does a good job running the company. In return, Harvey will forever recommend that Tom, Dick and Harry be reappointed to the board—thus guaranteeing that they continue to receive an easy eighty grand a year (a typical fee handed out to serve on a Fortune 500 corporate board) for doing very little work.

From the hypothetical, let's move to a real world example, and take a look at our old friend Gary Winnick and the company he led into bankruptcy, Global Crossing. According to a 2002 *Los Angeles Times* article, most of the directors who served on Global Crossing's board also had "economic or social ties to the company or its founder, Gary Winnick. Those who weren't employed directly by Global Crossing often did business with the company or Winnick's private investment firm, Pacific Capital Group."[42] On top of appointing his cronies to the board, Winnick also made certain that Global Cross-ing's board members didn't spend too much time actually looking into the operations of the company, as the board only met in person on a quarterly basis, their meetings typically beginning "with a din-ner, followed by a three-hour meeting the next morning. The board often would adjourn after lunch. About one-third of the meeting would be spent discussing the company's financial health."[43] And, following the high pay for little output theme, while being a Global Crossing board member didn't require much time or effort, it was still quite a lucrative endeavor, as "12 board members made more than $991 million buying and selling Global Crossing stock" after the company went public.[44]

Gary Winnick was far from the only CEO engaged in this type of board cronyism. Another chief executive who makes sure that he has loyal allies on his board is Fred Smith of FedEx. In Smith's case, he has tapped many long-time Fed Ex colleagues to serve on the company's board, all of whom he can count on not to threaten his leadership and certainly not his compensation. In return, these board members can rely on Smith to spread his corporate largesse in their direction, as each FedEx board member is paid a quarterly retainer of nearly $20,000.[45] In addition, each board member earns a fee to attend board meetings, as well as the ability to acquire stock options. The total cost to the company for all of this in 2008 was $2,664,410, according to the Corporate Library.

Among the FedEx board members who have stepped up to Smith's corporate trough are:

- Peter S. Willmott, who serves as the chairman of the board's Nominating and Governance Committee, which controls the make-up of the board and is supposed to act as a watch-dog over the CEO and the rest of management. Willmott served in various senior management positions at FedEx from 1974 to 1983, including a stint as President and Chief Operating Office.

- James L. Barksdale, who has had a seat on the board for nine years, previously served side by side with Smith in various senior management positions from 1979 to 1992, including Executive Vice President and Chief Operating Officer. FedEx has also donated to tax-exempt organizations for which Barksdale or his wife serve as a trustee or director.[46]

- J.R. Hyde, III who, along with David J. Bronczek, President and CEO of FedEx, serves on the board of Memphis Tomorrow, a nonprofit organization that links up top business leaders and Memphis government and civic officials. In 2008, FedEx shelled out a cool $1 million to Memphis Tomorrow, which is more than 25 percent of the organization's annual revenues.[47] FedEx has also promised to continue donating $1 million to Memphis Tomorrow's annually for the next five years.

While there has been a movement over the past few years to "break up the old boys' club and make boards less deferential" to the CEO, these attempts have largely failed. James Westphal, who teaches business at the University of Michigan, has discovered that even so-called "independent" board members are still unlikely to challenge the rule of the CEO because these members are generally nominated by either the CEO or other board members, who "tend to prefer directors who will be cheerleaders for the firm and won't rock the boat."[48]

More For The CEO Equals Less for the Workers

While complaint boards are certainly a boon for CEO compensation, they have an extremely detrimental effect on the salaries and pensions of regular workers. Continuing with our example of FedEx, while Fred Smith has been getting richer and richer thanks to his friendly board, the pay of his workers has been going in the opposite direction. In 2001, couriers at FedEx were paid an average of $16.92 per hour; during the same year, Smith made more than $2.2 million in pay and bonuses (not including his stock option grants), an hourly rate of $1,100, or 64 times the hourly wage of a courier. In 2002, while the average pay for a courier went up less than a dollar to $17.89 per hour, Smith's pay jumped to $2.7 million—an hourly rate of $1,337, almost 75 times the hourly wage of a courier.[49] In 2008, while the hourly rate of a courier had dropped to $17.14, Smith's total compensation was more than $13.5 million, over 750 times the hourly rate of a courier.[50] And, as if FedEx workers weren't getting enough of a raw deal, Smith decided in June 2008 to end the company's defined-benefit pension plan.[51]

It is no coincidence that as CEO pay has gone up, the number of real pensions for average workers has declined. After all, there is only so much cash in the corporate till—and if the CEO vacuums up the lion's share of that money, there is not much left for the rest of the employees. Since 1978, the number of defined-benefit plans has plummeted from 128,041 plans covering some 41 percent of private-sector workers, to 26,000, according to the Employee Benefit Research Institute.[52] In addition, the Bureau of Labor Statistics found that only 21 percent of workers in the private sector currently have defined-benefit pension plans.[53] Worse than that, in 2005, only 55 percent of full-time and part-time private sector workers worked at firms that sponsored any kind of retirement plan—whether it was the casino-type 401(k) or a defined-benefit pension—and only 45 percent participated in an employer-sponsored plan.[54] This compares with a 60 percent employer-sponsorship rate and 50 percent employee participation rate back in 2000.[55]

All this shows how we have gone from a country where workers, after putting in their time punching the clock, could at least count on a regular check during their retirement, to a country where it is a crapshoot whether retired workers can even pay their bills from month to month. However, CEOs have no such worries. For example, Fred Smith and other FedEx executives have a "Management Retention Agreement" that outlines a three-year employment agreement following a merger or acquisition, meaning they can't get fired even if the company is sold. And, if a new CEO did want to fire Smith, he would have to pay him a $26.6 million golden parachute.[56] Of course, no such protections exist for workers at the company.

7. The Wage Cupboard Is Bare

Your parents or grandparents have probably told you the story: how there was once a bedrock promise in this country that if you worked hard and kept your nose clean, you could earn a decent day's wage for a decent day's work. It's like Bruce Springsteen sang in his song "The Promised Land": "I've done my best to live the right way, I get up every morning and go to work each day." From the end of World War II up through the 1970s, the words of the Boss rang true for a majority of Americans: if they worked hard, they would receive a fair wage for their efforts.

In our current era of audacious greed, all that has changed. Therefore, our picture of the looting of America cannot be complete without an account of how a systematic three decades long wage and benefit theft has gone hand in glove—and, in fact, financed—the corporate robbery of this country.

We start with a simple idea: When workers produce more—either tangible products or services—than they did previously, they are being more efficient. This in turn usually means greater profit for a corporation. Historically, in addition to helping the corporate bottom line, increased efficiency has flowed back to workers in the form of higher wages. From the end of World War II through the mid 1970s, "the real wages of American workers nearly doubled, moving up in tandem with the growth in productivity."[1]

Over the past thirty years, however, the link between productivity gains and wages has been shattered. Since 1980, while productivity has grown more than 70 percent, the wages of non-managerial workers has remained flat (wages for the lowest-paid workers have actually gone down).[2] If not workers, then who is benefiting from the continuing increases in productivity? I am sure you guessed it already—the corporate elite. According to the Economic Policy Institute, while productivity grew almost three times faster than wages from 2001 through 2005, 70 percent of the nation's income growth during that time went straight into corporate coffers as profits—presumably to continue financing staggering pay and benefits for executives—a complete reversal from the seven previous business cycles, when 77 percent of the overall income growth went to wages.[3]

As the numbers reveal, we have basically lived through two distinct economic periods in this country since World War II. First, from right after the war until the mid-1970s, when productivity and wages basically tracked one other. That is, people worked hard and were productive—and that hard work was rewarded in ever increasing paychecks. Starting in the mid-1970s, however, while people kept working hard and productivity continued to soar, wage growth ceased. According to Joel Rogers, Director of the Center on Wisconsin Strategy, a progressive policy institute located on the campus of the University of Wisconsin-Madison, had wages continued to track productivity, the median family income in the United States today would be about $20,000 higher.[4] Furthermore, taking into account productivity, the minimum wage today should be $19.12 per hour, which would make it almost 50 percent above today's median wage.[5]

If you look at the most recent time period as an example, the recovery from the 2001 "mild" recession through the 2008 economic crash, the numbers are even more stark: while productivity went up by 16 percent, real wages and earnings increased by only 2 percent. That made it the first "recovery" on record that not only left the median family income below the level it had stood pre-recession (a decline of $2,000), but also left it even lower than it had been during the recession (a decline of $1,000).[6] Joel Rogers sums it all up quite simply, yet powerfully: "It's fair to say that most American workers today are making substantially less than the (historically, productivity-normed) wage of the economy's worst-off workers of a generation ago."

This emptying of the wage cupboard has had a devastating effect on the average American worker, essentially creating a two-tiered earnings system made up of the very rich and the rest of us:

- The top earners' share of wages, which was stable from the mid-1940s through the 1970s, nearly doubled from 1979 through 2006, from 7.3 percent to 13.6 percent. This is the result of earnings growth of 144.4 percent for the top 1 percent of earners over the past thirty years, compared to just 15.6 percent growth for the bottom 90 percent.[7]
- Those in the upper 0.1 percent of wage earners have hit the jackpot, as their annual earnings have grown 324 percent since 1979, to over $2.2 million in 2006. As a result, the earnings of the top 0.1 percent of Americans are now 77 times greater than the earnings of the bottom 90 percent, whereas in 1979 it was just 21 times as much.[8]
- The share of our national income hoarded by the top one percent was, as of 2006, 22.1 percent (a rise of three percentage points from 2004.)[9] The last time it was that high was in 1928 (23.9 percent)—just as the Great Depression was about to hit with its full fury.

With a higher percentage of wages going to the top one percent of earners, workers at the very bottom have been pushed down even further. As of 2007, 26.4 percent of Americans were earning poverty-level wages. These numbers include 34 percent of African American workers and 41.8 percent of Hispanic workers. (In addition, women were more likely to earn poverty level wages than men—31.4 percent vs. 21.8 percent).[10] To show you how this effects regular Americans, if a person being paid the current minimum wage of $7.25 an hour worked forty hours a week, every week, with no vacations, no holidays, no health care and no pension, he or she would earn the grand sum of $15,080. To put that amount into perspective, according to the U.S. Department of Health and Human Services, the 2009 poverty level for an individual is $10,800; for a family of three, $18,300.[11] So, someone working a full-time job at the current minimum wage would earn $4,280 more than poverty wages, assuming he or she worked 52 weeks a year, never took a day off and never got sick. And, things have actually improved greatly for low-paid workers over the past three years; if you go back to 2006, for example, at the end of a period where the minimum wage hadn't been raised in a decade, the difference between the poverty level and someone working full-time for the minimum wage was $418.[12]

Beyond the simple unfairness of the current system, wage inequality also tears at the country's social fabric because an economic system cannot endure if it fails to deliver a rising standard of living for a majority of its citizens. Stephen Roach, then Chief Economist and Director of Global Economic Analysis for Morgan Stanley, wrote in 2005 that, "American workers, long accustomed to receiving their 'just reward' as defined by their marginal productivity contribution, are facing the most profound disappointment of the modern era." He went on to add that, "The extraordinary stagnation of earned labor income in the past four years reflects a fundamental breakdown of the relationship between worker pay and productivity." Roach and others in the financial elite were worried, correctly it turned out, that the breakdown between worker pay and productivity did not bode well for the economy since consumers, weighed down by debt, were being forced to rely on assets like price-inflated homes. That, Roach said back in 2005, was unsustainable, both economically and politically.

So, truly, the story of the financial crisis of 2008 was not only the greed and incompetence of the corporate financial elite, but also the thirty-year long suppression of the wages of the American worker.

With no real wage gains over the past three decades, workers had no choice but to live off plastic—credit card after credit card—to finance basic living needs, health care and other expenses. When the credit ran out, a lot of people turned to the only other asset they had—their homes, which were over-inflated in value because of the real estate bubble. Once the bubble collapsed, there was nowhere else for people to go—and therefore consumer spending dried up, the economy drying up along with it.

The Beast of Bentonville

Nothing illustrates the wage cupboard is bare syndrome we have experienced over the past three decades better than the Beast of Bentonville, also known as Wal-Mart. The company has become a symbol for the divide between rich and poor in America, the suppression of workers' wages and the looting of the country's wealth and resources. Wal-Mart has long used "free market" rhetoric as a cover to leech off the public commons, while its owners have taken corporate thievery to a new level as the company has gone from community to community, feeding off the poverty of workers and consumers alike.[13]

On the one hand, you have America's richest family, the Waltons. As of September 2008, the four children of Wal-Mart founder Sam Walton—Alice, Christy, Jim and S. Robson—were collectively worth more than $90 billion (though their fortune has probably been slightly reduced with the decline in the company's stock since over the past year), placing each of them on the top ten list of richest Americans.[14] On the other hand, behind that wealth is a sordid tale of lawsuits, and a trail of poverty, exploitation and abuse, much of it built around the company's signature tactic, union-busting. "Wal-Mart workers have virtually no chance to organize because they're up against unfair US labor laws and a giant company that will do just about anything to keep unions out," said Carol Pier, senior researcher on labor rights and trade for Human Rights Watch, the globally recognized independent rights monitor. "That one-two punch devastates workers' right to form and join unions."[15]

In 2007, Human Rights Watch released an in-depth investigation of Wal-Mart, which found that the company "begins to indoctrinate workers and managers to oppose unions from the moment they are hired." Toward this end, managers at the company are provided with a "Manager's Toolkit," which offers them steps on how to "remain union free" in the event union organizers choose their store as their next target. If workers do in fact succeed in organizing, store managers are required to report that activity to Wal-Mart's Union Hotline; the company will respond by sending out its Labor Relations Team to crush the organizing efforts.

In addition, Human Rights Watch also found that Wal-Mart engages in a slew of illegal anti-union activities, including having managers eavesdrop on employees; the use of surveillance cameras to monitor union supporters; telling workers they will lose their benefits if they organize; and "prohibiting union flyer distribution, while allowing discussion of other issues and circulation of non-union materials." The company has also disciplined "union supporters for policy violations that it has let slide for union opponents," as well as illegally firing workers for getting involved in union activity. [16]

As a consequence of the company's anti-union imitation tactics, workers at Wal-Mart are convinced that they will suffer "dire consequences if they form a union," including retaliation, or loss of their jobs. Employees of the meat-cutting department at a store in Texas certainly experienced these dire consequences first hand back in 2000 when they voted to join a union. The response of Wal-Mart was to shut down the entire department—as well as every other meat-cutting department in the region, affecting 180 stores in 6 states.[17] The Walton family wasn't going to take any chance that the "virus" of unionization might spread among its meat-cutters. Currently, not a single Wal-Mart store in the United States is unionized.

A Cancer in the Community

The supposed allure of shopping at Wal-Mart is that consumers love its low prices and therefore save tons of money by shopping there. However, this "free market" mythology cannot hide some basic truths about the company. In 2006, the Economic Policy Institute put out a paper—co-authored by Jared Bernstein, currently Chief Economist and Economic Policy Adviser to Vice President Joseph Biden—which examined the argument that in order to have low prices, workers at Wal-Mart had to be paid low wages. Among the report's conclusions were:

- A study conducted by the consulting firm Global Insight which concluded that Wal-Mart's expansion had saved U.S. consumers $263 billion was deeply flawed, as the "statistical analysis generating this widely quoted figure fails the most rudimentary sensitivity checks used in good economic analysis, rendering its conclusions unreliable."
- A robust set of research findings revealed that Wal-Mart's entry into local labor markets reduced the pay of workers in competing stores. This effect was largest in the south, where Wal-Mart's expansion has been the greatest.
- Wal-Mart could raise wages and benefits for its workers significantly without raising prices, yet still earn a healthy profit. For example, while still maintaining a profit margin almost 50 percent greater than Costco, a key competitor, Wal-Mart could have raised the wages and benefits of each one of its non-supervisory employees in 2005 by more than $2,000 without having to raise its prices a single penny.[18]

Taken as a whole, the report revealed how Wal-Mart overstates its benefit to consumers while understating how badly it hurts workers by offering substandard wages. In fact, Wal-Mart actually raises poverty levels. A 2004 study conducted by Penn State, "Wal-Mart and County-Wide Poverty" found that 20,000 families nationwide had fallen below the poverty rate as a result of the invasion of Wal-Mart stores into their communities.[19] The study concluded that Wal-Mart "unequivocally raised family poverty rates in US counties during the 1990s relative to places that had no such stores." Wal-Mart does this in three ways:

1. Poverty rates rise when retail workers displaced from existing mom-and-pop type operations work for Wal-Mart at lower wages because they have no other alternative.
2. Even though Wal-Mart presents itself to communities as a "good local citizen" and often engages in local philanthropy through the Sam Walton Foundation, this type of philanthropy "may not be as extensive or effective as that which the displaced mom-and-pop type stores would have provided."
3. By destroying the local class of entrepreneurs, "the Wal-Mart chain also destroys local leadership capacity."

In addition to wage abuse, Wal-Mart is also notorious for abusing and mistreating its workers. You could spend a whole day trying to keep track of the legal actions pending against Wal-Mart, spread out across the country. Just to provide you with a taste:

- Wal-Mart discriminated against its female employees in terms of promotions and pay raises, and, as a result, is currently facing the largest sex discrimination case in U.S. history. The plaintiffs estimate they could "win billions of dollars in lost pay and damages and that as many as two million women who have worked for Wal-Mart in its American stores since 1998 could join the suit."[20]
- In December 2008, a state judge in Minnesota ruled that Wal-Mart had forced workers to work off-the-clock and had barred workers from having full rest periods and breaks for meals in violation of state wage and hour laws. The judge said that, "Wal-Mart's failure to compensate plaintiffs was willful...Wal-Mart was on notice from numerous sources

of the wage and hour violations at issue and failed to correct the problem.'" The company didn't break the law once or twice or even 100 times—the judge ruled that Wal-Mart had broken the law 2 million times, and ordered a $6.5 million back-pay judgment. And Wal-Mart actually lucked out, because if the case had gone to a jury trial, with $1,000 penalties for each violation, even the billionaire Walton's might have squealed a bit at having to come up with $2 billion to pay the judgment.[21]

- In January 2007, Wal-Mart made a deal to pay $33 million in back pay to tens of thousands of workers for wages that should have been paid over the previous five years.[22]

Putting a human force on these numbers is Debbie Shank. In May 2000, a minivan driven by Shank, who was an employee of Wal-Mart at the time, was broadsided by a truck. Shank survived the accident, but suffered significant brain damage, requiring permanent around-the-clock care in a nursing home. Though Shank was covered by her Wal-Mart health insurance plan, it wasn't enough to cover all of her medical expenses. Shank filed a lawsuit against the company whose truck had hit her minivan, which was settled for approximately $1 million. After legal fees, Shank was left with $417,000. At that point, Wal-Mart sued Shank for $470,000, the amount the company had paid for her medical care. Since the health plan actually allowed the company to sue its employees for damages they received in court, the law was actually on Wal-Mart's side.[23] However, the company was shamed by a national campaign that spread through the grassroots and onto national television, and eventually gave up trying to collect the money.[24]

The case of Debbie Shank shows the immense gap between how Wal-Mart actually treats its workers, versus its claim to be a "good, local citizen." This gap becomes even greater when we consider the company's treatment of workers like Debbie Shank in light of the personal priorities of Alice Walton. What would you do if you were, along with your mother, the richest woman in the world, but your workers either couldn't afford health insurance or had to pay through the nose to get pathetic insurance? Of course you would buy a painting that cost more than $35 million.[25] Alice Walton—who, at the time was tied with her now-deceased mother for the 13th spot on *Forbes* magazine's list of the wealthiest people in the world with a worth of $18 billion—bought an Asher B. Durand painting called "Kindred Spirits," which was to be displayed in the Walton family museum, scheduled to open in 2009 in Bentonville. While Alice was splurging on art, most of her workers couldn't even afford health insurance.

One of the great frauds that Wal-Mart perpetrates is that it is a paragon of the so-called "free market." In truth, the company's model of low wages and cheap prices could not survive without broad government support, not the least of which is for health care, as most Wal-Mart workers cannot afford the bare bones, pathetic health care the company offers. For example, in 2003, Wal-Mart employees paid 41 percent of their insurance premium costs, compared to 10 percent for workers at Costco. (The national average was 16 percent for single coverage and 27 percent for family coverage.)[26] That is where the public subsidy comes in, as folks in Ohio discovered when the state spent $111.5 million in 2007 to cover the costs of Medicaid for 111,000 workers and their dependents from the fifty companies with the highest enrollment in the program. Surprise: Wal-Mart led the pack of Medicaid enrollees, with a monthly average of 13,141 employees and dependents.[27] As Susan Chambers, Executive Vice President for Benefits at Wal-Mart, wrote in a 2005 memo to the company's Board of Directors, "…our critics are correct in some of their observations. Specifically, our coverage is expensive for low-income families, and Wal-Mart has a significant percentage of Associates and their children on public assistance."[28]

This is nothing new for Wal-Mart, as the company depends on taxpayer-financed health care to keep their workers from dropping dead or being chronically ill. According to the website Wake Up

Wal-Mart, "In 2005, nearly 300,000 Wal-Mart workers and their family members depended on taxpayer-funded public health care at an estimated total cost to American taxpayers of $1.37 billion." It was predicted that the "Wal-Mart health care crisis will cost taxpayers an estimated $9.1 billion over the next five years."[29]

Of course, all this assumes that an employee at Wal-Mart even has health insurance. While 64 percent of workers in very large firms (defined as 5,000 employees or more) receive their health benefits from their employer, Wal-Mart only covers about half of its employees. In addition, Wal-Mart workers cannot get health insurance until they have been employed by the company for six months; the average at most retail employers is three months. And part-time workers cannot get health coverage until they have been employed for a year—and since most part-time workers do not stay at Wal-Mart for a year, most of them are never covered.[30]

The Wal-Mart 22

In addition to abusing its employees, Wal-Mart also abuses the individual states that are often so anxious to have the company open up stores within their jurisdictions. In 2007, the *Wall Street Journal* discovered that in twenty-five states, Wal-Mart had been essentially paying rent on its stores not to the state government, but to itself, and then deducting that amount from the state taxes it owed. The way the scheme worked was that a Wal-Mart subsidiary would pay rent to a real-estate investment trust, or REIT, which is entitled to a tax break if it paid its profits out in dividends. The REIT was usually owned by another Wal-Mart subsidiary, which received the REIT's dividends tax-free. Wal-Mart then deducted the rent from the state taxes it owed as a "business expense" even though no money had ever left the company's coffers.[31] While Wal-Mart claimed at the time that it was "in compliance with federal and state tax laws,"[32] in January 2008, a judge in North Carolina ruled against the company, writing in his decision that "There is no evidence that the rent transaction, taken as a whole, has any real economic substance apart from its beneficial effect on plaintiffs' North Carolina tax liability."[33]

This scam had been proposed to Wal-Mart by the accounting firm of Ernst & Young after Wal-Mart had put out the word in 2001 that it wanted to find "creative" ways to cut its state tax bills. As a result, in 2002, Ernst & Young delivered to Wal-Mart "a 37-page proposal laying out a smorgasbord of 27 potential tax strategies, most tailored to a particular state's tax code. It described one of them as 'a very aggressive strategy with considerable risk.'"[34] Among the places where Wal-Mart took an "aggressive" stance was in California, where the company took tax deductions for dividends it hadn't actually paid, and in Texas, where Ernst & Young advised Wal-Mart that it could "exploit a wrinkle in the tax law involving limited partners from out-of-state—a maneuver subsequently shut down by the state's legislature."[35] Wal-Mart was so aggressive in the Golden State that California's Franchise Tax Board put one of the company's tax-avoidance strategies on its list of "Abusive Tax Shelters."[36]

Based on Wal-Mart's horrific treatment of both its workers and the states where it sets up shop, why would any politician who purports him or herself to be a defender of the working person want to be affiliated with the company? The answer is simple—"The Club," as we explored before, is a very powerful force, and it is often deployed on behalf of Wal-Mart. For an example of this clubby relationship, let's take a look at the Wal-Mart 22, the 22 *Democrats*— Marion Berry (AR), Sanford Bishop (GA), Dan Boren (OK), G. K. Butterfield (NC), James Clyburn (SC), Bud Cramer (AL), Henry Cuellar (TX), Artur Davis (AL), Diana DeGette (CO), Harold Ford (TN)—now a former Representative having failed in his 2006 Senate bid—Charles Gonzalez (TX), Ron Kind (WI), Jim Matheson (UT), Dennis Moore (KS), Mike Ross (AR), John Salazar (CO), Vic Snyder (AR), John Tanner (TN), Mike Thompson (CA), Bennie Thompson (MS), Ed Towns (NY), and Al Wynn (MD)—also a former Representative having lost his seat in a 2008 Democratic primary—*who, on June 24, 2005, voted against an amendment to the 2006 fiscal year labor appropriations bill (offered by Rosa DeLauro, Democrat of Connecticut) that would have barred the Department of Labor from spending money to implement part of a deal it had made with Wal-Mart calling for advance notice of inspections any time the department planned to investigate the company for child labor violations.

This "deal" had come about after Wal-Mart stores in Connecticut, New Hampshire and Arkansas had been found guilty of systematically violating child labor laws by allowing workers under the age of eighteen to operate dangerous machinery like cardboard balers, forklifts and chain saws.[37] For violating child labor laws, the U.S. government had reached a "deal" with Wal-Mart wherein the company was fined a measly $135,540 and the government agreed to give the company "15 days' notice before investigating any stores facing complaints of child labor violations."[38] Wal-Mart was also allowed to avoid fines altogether "if it brought stores into compliance within 10 days of being notified of violations."[39] Wal-Mart was essentially being told by the government, "Next time we want to investigate any laws you might be in the process of breaking, we're going to tell you about the investigation beforehand"—giving the company ample time to cover its tracks, shred documents or muddle the trail. After criticism from some Congressional Democrats, labor groups and the Department of Labor's Inspector General, the inspection deal was allowed to expire in January of 2006.[40]

The bottom line, however, was that Wal-Mart endangered the lives of children and got away with a fine of $135,540 (and almost got away with a two week investigation pre-notification). Does anyone have a calculator handy in order to figure out what percentage

---

*I'd like to note one thing about the Wal-Mart 22. A disturbing number of them were, and are, members of the Congressional Black Caucus (Bishop, Butterfield, Clyburn, Davis, Bennie Thompson, Towns and the now former Representatives Ford and Wynn).

that financial "penalty" represents to a company that had sales of $375 billion in 2007?[41] Unfortunately, we have a system in America that encourages companies to violate the law because it's a very small cost of their doing business. And even if investigators descended like vultures on Wal-Mart's Bentonville headquarters, the company will happily continue to write checks for $135,540 in order to keep the registers humming and the cash piling up.

In reality, crimes against workers will never stop until we start putting corporate executives in jail for committing such crimes— not just for stock manipulation and accounting fraud. How fast do you think Wal-Mart would clean up its act—stop violating child labor laws, stop illegally firing workers who try to unionize, stop discriminating against women—if former Wal-Mart CEO Lee Scott had been put in jail at the time of the aforementioned violations, or if one of the Walton billionaires had to spend a few days, weeks or months (I won't be so naïve as to suggest years) in the pokey? Indeed, our standards for crimes against people at work verge on the hypocritical. Outside of the workplace, endangering the welfare of a child can land a parent in jail. We also easily pass laws for drug crimes, and in some states like my own New York, we put people behind bars for life terms if the crime they've committed is a third offense—crimes that are often less severe than the work-related injuries caused by companies like Wal-Mart. However, under "Club" rules, giant corporations like Wal-Mart are allowed to pay $135,540 for the privilege of violating child labor laws because of the able assistance of politicians like the Wal-Mart 22. It reminds me of the scene in *The Untouchables* when Eliot Ness, sure he has a slam dunk case against Al Capone, finds out that the entire jury has been bribed. Of course, the movie ends with a happy resolution, but we aren't in Hollywood when it comes to the basic rights of workers—this script is real and the outcome has a harmful effect on millions of peoples' lives.

Republican or Democrat: Both Friends of Wal-Mart

The votes of the Wal-Mart 22 show the connections that Wal-Mart has long had to the highest levels of power—within both political parties. For example, in 2005, the company set up a "war room" to attack its opponents which was staffed by both Republican and Democratic operatives, including Michael K. Deaver, who helped shape the image of Ronald Reagan, and Leslie Dach, a veteran of media work for Bill Clinton.[42] For those of you who might recoil at the notion that one of Bill Clinton's media consultants was working for Wal-Mart, understand that the Clintons have had a very tight relationship with Wal-Mart going back to the days when Bill Clinton was governor of Arkansas. Hillary Clinton even sat on Wal-Mart's board for six years—at a time when the company was deeply engaged in anti-union activities—and only left the board when her husband was preparing to run for president.

The Clinton's ties with Wal-Mart underscore the often incestuous relationship between the corporate world and the political sphere, no matter which party someone belongs to as under our current campaign finance system, you are required to belly up to the bar and take corporate cash whether you are a Republican or a Democrat. Beyond the campaign finance issue, the Clinton's relationship with Wal-Mart—as well as the actions of the Wal-Mart 22—shows how there is often little difference between Republicans and Democrats when it comes to pro-corporate behavior. As hypocritical as the worst Republican, a Democrat can say that he or she is pro-environment and pro-worker, and yet not have any issue working with a company like Wal-Mart, which has the biggest negative impact of any single company on the environment, not to mention on the life of its workers.

And if you happen to think that I am unfairly singling out what is just a tiny portion of the Democratic Party, how about this: By 2008, the Democratic Party had drawn almost even with the Republican Party in terms of the money it received from Wal-Mart, according to the Center for Responsive Politics. The Center's data showed that in the twelve years prior to the 2008 election cycle, Wal-Mart's PAC had given 98 percent of its money to Republicans. In the 2008 cycle, however, Democrats received 48 percent of Wal-Mart's PAC expenditures.[43] The list of Democrats who received money in the 2008 cycle was breathtaking in its scope, spanning what the traditional political chattering class calls "liberals", "moderates", and "conservatives" and included 18 of the Wal-Mart 22 (out of the 21 who were still in office at the time), as well as Senators' Max Baucus (D-MT), Mary Landrieu (D-LA), Claire McCaskill (D-MO), and, naturally, both senators from Arkansas, Democrats Blanche Lincoln and Mark Pryor. What you have are elected officials hailing from a party that proclaims itself to be on the side of working people taking money from a serial labor and child law violator.

One of the reasons Wal-Mart has been increasing its level of donations to Democrats is because the company is trying to buy the loyalty of elected political leaders in order to undercut passage of the Employee Free Choice Act. Wal-Mart fears that if EFCA is passed, it will unleash a wave of unionizing in its stores. In addition to greasing the palms of politicians, Wal-Mart has also been leaning on its own managers and supervisors, conducting intensive "educational" meetings on the subject of EFCA, as well as having pushed company employees to vote Republican in the 2008 election. "The meeting leader said, 'I am not telling you how to vote, but if the Democrats win, this bill will pass and you won't have a vote on whether you want a union,'" said a Wal-Mart customer-service supervisor from Missouri. "I am not a stupid person. They were telling me how to vote."[44]

Putting aside the point about whether Wal-Mart's internal political electioneering was legal under federal election law, the far bigger issue was that the company was making it clear that it would spare no effort to defeat EFCA. Wal-Mart's PAC spending on Democratic candidates is aimed at one thing: to make sure that EFCA does not pass and, if it does pass, to make sure that the bill that reaches President Obama's desk will be severely weakened.

"40 percent of 12 years ago"

We are now moving into an era in which something unprecedented in the history of this country is occurring. As summed up by *The Wall Street Journal*, "Pay cuts, rather than layoffs, have emerged as an alternative way for many companies to reduce labor costs as demand slumps during the recession."[45] Thus, as we climb out of our current economic mess over the coming years, we will emerge into a totally remade landscape. While many people may eventually return to work and unemployment might decline—at least as measured by government statistics, which don't tell the whole story—the number who are out of work might ultimately not become the most accurate description of how much working people are hurting. Instead, if you continue to cut wages, and people can't survive on their paychecks (paychecks that have been shrinking for three decades), you will be effectively creating a brand new world where people won't be able to make ends meet even if they are working, as their wages will not be able to keep up with increasing costs.

I found many examples of this new "trend" when I posted a diary about the pay cut phenomena on Daily Kos in June 2009. One woman posted a comment, saying, "My daughter, who is a professor at a college that shall not be named, called me yesterday and told me that her pay, and that of her peers, has been cut by 18%, by the state Governor [sic]...My daughter is very angry, but relates that since she HAS to work, she is not in any position to fight the cuts. She is very depressed, being that she and her husband have a son who will be entering college next year, and money is an issue for them right now. She is also angry that the school did not cut their workload by 18%." Another commenter flatly declared, when speaking of his pay: "I'm at 40 percent of 12 years ago."[46]

Ultimately, this trend toward lower pay is not simply reflective of a hiccup in the economy, during which people might be a little short for awhile before returning to their old level of financial security once things return to normal. Instead, what is going on, and has been going on for the past three decades, is nothing less than the elite knocking the working class down another peg on the economic ladder. I'm sure Wal-Mart is proud.

8. The Great Collapse

Let's start at the end of the story. On September 29, 2008, the Dow Jones Industrial Average fell 777 points, the largest one day drop in its history. The sell-off was so complete that just 162 stocks went up in value, while 3,073 declined.[1] In monetary terms, $1.2 trillion was lost in a single day.[2] And that was just the tip of the iceberg: by mid-October, the market had dropped an additional 20 percent, leaving it with an overall decline of over 40 percent from its high in October of 2007. Adding in the $3.3 trillion that was lost because of the decline of home values,[3] and the American economy lost approximately $10 trillion in 2008—with at least another $2 trillion worth of home equity value likely to vanish over the next couple of years.[4]

The traditional press referred to this wealth destruction using adjectives such as "earthquake" or "tsunami." But those kinds of descriptions were way off base because they gave the impression of a sudden, unforeseeable natural disaster that could not have been predicted or contained. In truth, the collapse of 2008 was predicted by many, but those predictions were roundly ignored. For example, in May 2006, Michael Hudson, Distinguished Research Professor of Economics at the University of Missouri, Kansas City wrote a piece in *Harper's* about the coming crash in the housing market: "The bubble will burst, and when it does, the people who thought they would be living the easy life of a landlord will soon find that what they really signed up for was the hard servitude of debt serfdom."[5] Similarly, on September 7, 2006, Nouriel Roubini, an economics professor at New York University, in an address to the International Monetary Fund, warned that the United States was likely to face a "once-in-a-lifetime housing bust, an oil shock, sharply declining consumer confidence and, ultimately, a deep recession." Roubini laid out a harrowing sequence of events: "homeowners defaulting on mortgages, trillions of dollars of mortgage-backed securities unraveling worldwide and the global financial system shuddering to a halt." All this, he said, "could cripple or destroy hedge funds, investment banks and other major financial institutions like Fannie Mae and Freddie Mac." The reaction of his audience at the IMF? "The audience seemed skeptical, even dismissive. As Roubini stepped down from the lectern after his talk, the moderator of the event quipped, 'I think perhaps we will need a stiff drink after that.'" And when economist Anirvan Banerji delivered his response to the speech, "he noted that Roubini's predictions did not make use of mathematical models and dismissed his hunches as those of a career naysayer."[6]

Indeed, in those heady pre-collapse days, anyone who dared to even suggest that the economy would soon be in trouble was dismissed as if they were raining on a party that would just keep on going and going. Feeding this frenzy were the CEOs at the top of the food chain, whose web of greed ensnared this country, ultimately driving it into the crisis we all experienced in 2008, and that many of us are still living through today.

The Countywide Crisis

No one better represents the audacity of greed that got this country into the economic crisis than Angelo Mozilo, the CEO of Countrywide Financial from the company's beginnings in 1969 until July of 2008. From nothing, Mozilo built Countrywide into a "$500 billion home loan machine with 62,000 employees, 900 offices and assets of $200 billion." On the backs of desperate homeowners, Mozilo made himself a fortune, mainly on huge annual stock option grants; from 1984 through 2007, he pocketed $406 million by cashing in those options. However, he never showed much faith in his own company, failing to buy a single share in Countrywide after 1987. Instead, he was simply a leech on the company's equity. Indeed, as the company hit the rocks during the mushrooming subprime crisis in 2007, Mozilo was making sure that he would not personally take the financial hit that hundreds of thousands of his costumers were facing, as he pocketed a third of his $406 million overall stock options in 2006 and 2007.[7]

Mozilo, in fact, kept up his personal enrichment even as his company was falling apart. By the end of 2007, as the Countrywide crisis was spiraling out of control, Mozilo had tucked away $121.5 million by exercising stock options. He also banked $22.1 million in pay in 2007—a year when the company lost $704 million, its shares slid 79 percent and it cut 11,000 workers from its payroll.[8] So, while the customers, shareholders and workers of Countrywide were drowning, Mozilo was flying high.

In his defense, Mozilo offered the usual argument of the failed CEO: that he was just the innocent victim of a market gone bad. "It's easy to have hindsight" he said in an interview with *National Mortgage News* in October of 2007. "No one saw this coming. No one."[9] That, however, is either an outright lie, or the height of self-delusion. "In terms of being unresponsive to what was happening, to sticking it out the longest, and continuing to justify the garbage they were selling, Countrywide was the worst lender," said Ira Rheingold, executive director of the National Association of Consumer Advocates, in 2007. "And anytime states tried to pass responsible lending laws, Countrywide was fighting it tooth and nail."[10] More importantly, in many ways Countryside *was* the mortgage market, since, as the biggest player on the field, it set the standard that other companies followed. As one former executive with the company said, "Countrywide said it was meeting market conditions. But they were the largest mortgage originator in the country. How can you say that it is not you that is causing it, if in fact you dominate the market?"[11]

It went even deeper than that, as Mozilo encouraged so-called "affordability" loans that helped his company seize greater market share. These types of loans ginned up huge profits for Countrywide, raked in mainly from regular people who had to pay commissions on loans that they should not have been eligible for in the first place. The company was like a drug dealer, hooking people on something they desperately wanted, with no way out once they were addicted. Among the kinds of loans in this vein that the company gave out where "interest-only loans, which required borrowers to only pay the interest on the loan—they did not have to pay back the principal until later in the life of the mortgage." Countrywide was the number two originator of these loans in 2006 and 2007 (The top originator was Wells Fargo).[12] Countrywide also provided its customers with what were known as "pay option adjustable rate mortgages" which permitted borrowers to pay only a small percentage of the interest—and none of the principal—during an "introductory" period. While these loans lured borrowers in, they had serious repercussions. For example, if a borrower made just the minimum payment on his or her loan, their "mortgage would grow in size rather than fall. Another possible negative was that the borrower could eventually owe more than the home was worth." Pay option A.R.M.'s accounted for just 6 percent of Countrywide's mortgage originations in 2004; that figure had climbed to 19 percent by 2005. And these loans were where the big money was, as Countrywide made "gross profit margins of more than 4 percent on such loans, compared with 2 percent margins earned on loans backed by the Federal Housing Administration."[13] You actually had Countryside salespeople handing out these types of loans to borrowers even if they had twice failed to pay a current mortgage on time or were in bankruptcy or foreclosure on a previous property.

All this was driven by Mozilo's greed—as well as the greed of his board members. While Countrywide was snaring consumers, shackling them into unaffordable mortgages, the company's board made no move to harness the clearly out of control Mozilo. Wonder why? In 2006, the directors on Countrywide's board earned between

$345,000 to $539,000 each in cash, stock and other compensation—an incredibly generous payoff that most people would find a sufficient reason to keep their mouths shut.[14]

Freddie and Fannie...and Daniel and Richard and Dwight and Chad

Mozilo wasn't the only CEO who made off with a fortune while his customers and shareholders were suffering the consequences of the housing meltdown in 2007 and 2008. The song was much the same at Freddie Mac and Fannie Mae. In fact, the robbery at Freddie and Fannie was even more obscene because those two quasi-government institutions had been set up in order to help homeowners by providing a secondary market for mortgages. As a result, when you took out a mortgage with your bank, Freddie and Fannie were supposed to be there to buy up the mortgage as a type of gold standard guarantee.

However, the executives running the show at Freddie and Fannie were part of the same greed scheme that cratered the economy: rather than helping hardworking people get into the housing market, they instead wanted to enrich themselves, so they jumped right into the sub-prime casino. And they were not hurt one bit when everything went south, as the *Los Angeles Times* reported in 2008:

> Shareholders in Fannie Mae and Freddie Mac saw the value of their stock nearly disappear Monday after the mortgage giants had been taken over by the federal government, but the companies' chief executives will leave after banking millions and taking millions more on the way out the door... Fannie Mae's Daniel Mudd and Freddie Mac's Richard Syron stepped down but are helping with the transition of their companies into federal conservatorship under the Federal Housing Finance Agency. The agency has not said how much they will earn in their new roles. Mudd earned $11.6 million last year, and Syron made $18.3 million. In

both cases, a large portion of their pay packages included stock that was valued much higher at the end of 2007 than it was as of Monday, when it was trading at less than $1 a share. By conservative estimates, Mudd, 49, and Syron, 64, will leave with an additional $7.3 million and $6.3 million, respectively, as part of a severance package, according to an analysis by Paul Hodgson at the Corporate Library.[15]

Mudd and Syron were at the helm of two companies that effectively were in bankruptcy and had to be rescued by the federal government—and yet both walked away with a small fortune. And it wasn't simply that they mismanaged their companies; their behavior— rushing after fool's gold and exercising, at best, horrible judgment in leaping on the top of the housing bubble—ended up costing millions of people their homes and saddling them with years of crushing debt.

Overall, the 2008 economic crisis, while bad for most regular citizens, was a great time for CEOs to cash in—even as their home-building or financial service companies were going bankrupt or their shares were dropping like stones in water. A *Wall Street Journal* analysis in November 2008 found that fifteen of the CEOs deeply connected to the financial crisis had each banked more than $100 million from pay or stock sales over the previous five years. That elite group included the chiefs of Lehman Brothers and Bear Sterns, as well as two other executives whose companies' stock had dropped more than 90 percent from their high-water marks, or worse, had filed for bankruptcy. The study probed 120 public companies in sectors ranging from banking, mortgage finance, student lending, stock brokerage and home building—all industries that played a central role in the vanquishing of trillions of dollars in wealth in 2007 and 2008. Not surprisingly, that financial storm did not ruffle any of the top executives and directors of those firms who, *The Journal* found, collectively reaped a bounty of more than $21 billion.[16]

Wonder what you could buy with $21 billion? You could start

at the home of Dwight Schar, chairman of NVR Inc., a Reston, Virginia-based home builder. Among the lesser known executives who got in on the housing bubble, Schar must feel cramped in his $85.6 million, 11-acre oceanfront compound in Palm Beach, Florida, complete with a tennis court and two pools. Or how about R. Chad Dreier, chairman and chief executive of Ryland Group Inc., a Calabasas, California home builder who, according to *The Journal's* analysis, made $181 million during a five-year period—even though his company's stock price plummeted 85 percent from its high in 2005. In addition to a 4,900 square foot hilltop house in Santa Barbara, Dreier owns an office building that houses his "collection of baseball cards, sports memorabilia, gems, minerals and other items. State records say he owns several cars, including a 2004 Porsche coupe worth $448,000."

The top three executives at New Century Financial were feeding at the trough as well, handing out loans to people who simply stated that they could afford them—no documentation necessary. Their take from the legalized robbery: $74 million over four years, which helped the company's CEO, Robert Cole find comfort in a 9,200 square foot oceanfront home in Laguna Beach, California.

And while our analysis so far has been focused on the mortgage industry, not all the predatory corporate behavior that led to the financial meltdown was focused on prospective homeowners. The folks at First Marblehead made a killing on student loans, taking advantage of people who, once they had run out of cheaper government-backed loans, were forced into high-interest rate loans. As a result of the company's greed, life is pretty good for First Marblehead's CEO, Daniel Meyers, who pocketed $96 million from pay and stock sales from 2003 through 2007. He sure needed it too; how else could he have afforded the $10.3 million he used in 2004 to buy a 45-acre Spanish-style villa in Newport, Rhode Island. However, that still wasn't good enough for Meyers, who" tore down the villa and is constructing a five building, 38,000 square-foot compound called Seaward with a carriage house, a guest house and a caretaker's cottage."[17]

The culture of greed cascaded through every orifice of the financial elite. At financial giants like Merrill Lynch, the lure of piles of cash encouraged bond traders to cobble together extremely risky loan packages. It didn't matter if those loans went bad, bankrupting people and projects, as the bonuses paid out to the top brokers were salted away or spent by the time disaster struck—and no one was going to force those brokers to give back the money. "What happened to their investments was of no interest to them, because they would already be paid," said Paul Hodgson, senior research associate at the Corporate Library. In 2006 alone, 100 people in Merrill Lynch's bond department made "a buck"—which in cute financial parlance meant they made one million dollars. That same year, more than 50 lucky people at Goldman Sachs notched a cool $20 million each.[18]

...And let's not forget Kerry and Ken

Among the reckless corporate thieves who were responsible for the 2008 crash, Kerry Killinger, from 1990 through 2008 the CEO of Washington Mutual, once the nation's largest savings and loan institution, certainly stands out in the crowd. Killinger pushed WaMu into the risky sub-prime mortgage field with a vengeance, increasing the company's home-lending unit sales from $707 million in 2002 to almost $2 billion the following year. During the same period, WaMu was also heavily pushing adjustable rate mortgages, or ARMs. The ARMs were attractive because they offered low initial interest rates, and allowed borrowers to pay back as much or as little as they wanted each month. However, borrowers who paid the minimum were "underpaying the interest due and adding to their principal, eventually causing [their] loan payments to balloon."[19] For WaMu, the ARMs were a goldmine because they carried higher fees than other loans, allowing the company "to book profits on interest payments that borrowers deferred." And WaMu didn't worry about customers defaulting on their loans because "by the time loans went bad, they were often in other hands." ARMs expanded from about a quarter of new home loans at WaMu in 2003 to 70 percent by 2006. And Killinger was amply rewarded for that growth, receiving pay of $19 million in 2005 and $24 million in 2006.[20]

The gravy train kept rolling for Killinger, even as WaMu was falling apart in 2007 and 2008, cutting its quarterly dividend from 15 cents to a penny and dumping 3,000 workers.[21] The company's proxy statement for 2007 showed that Killinger was given a large grant of stock and options awards valued at close to $13 million—on top of his $1 million salary.[22] "This throws the whole concept of pay for performance out the window," said Rich Ferlauto, the Director of Pension and Benefit Policy for the American Federation of State, County and Municipal Employees (AFSCME). "Management of subprime risk was central to the obligations of the CEO and other top executives at Washington Mutual. So to take that out of the pay formula isn't a rational approach to allocating rewards. It seems that everyone is suffering except the executives who were directly responsible in some manner for the subprime crisis."[23]

In fact, while the company was going soft on Killinger, it was being hard on its customers who had fallen on tough times and were looking to get some relief on their mortgages. "I find Washington Mutual the most difficult when I try to negotiate forbearance agreements which are the last hope for people who are about to lose their homes," remarked Michael Sichenzia of Dynamic Consulting Enterprises, a Deerfield Beach, Florida company that offers homeowners help in avoiding foreclosure. "I would love to have them recognize that we have available candidates for workouts and forbearance, but they just aren't doing it."[24]

Ultimately, Killinger's story was the quintessential tale of the warping power of greed. He was described, at the beginning of his career as a modest man who, as he built his banking empire, flew coach and eliminated high-level perks at institutions that he took over. He even married his high-school sweetheart. Fast-forward to 2000: he had divorced his high-school sweetheart wife of 32 years (he would remarry the following year), built a $3.5 million, 4,.400 square-foot home in an upscale neighborhood and bought another $2 million home in the exclusive, golf course enclave of Palm Desert, California. In 2007, as WaMu was reporting massive losses and its stock was cratering, Killinger picked up a third home—because, after all, a real CEO can't make do with just two houses—for $6.4 million in Palm Desert, nestled in the ultra-exclusive Bighorn Golf Club community. According to press reports, "Killinger, who once stripped companies of executive perks, was growing accustomed to them. He started using corporate jets, racking up $232,484 in personal jet use, not related to WaMu business, between 2003 and 2006, according to regulatory filings."[25]

In the end, the crash of WaMu was as spectacular as its rise during the subprime era. On September 26, 2008 the company filed for bankruptcy—one day after federal regulators grabbed its assets and sold them to JPMorgan Chase for $1.9 billion. In its wake, WaMu left a tax bill of $12.5 billion—as well as a lot of angry people.[26] In February 2009, a New Mexico man was arrested for sending death threats to sixty-five different banks in envelopes containing a white powder that turned out to be harmless. He told police he had acted because he was mad about the more than $60,000 he had lost when WaMu went belly-up.[27] While not everyone took such extreme steps, the stories were still heartbreaking. Tedda Hughes, who, with her husband Benjamin, invested her life savings of $27,000 in WaMu, told *ABC News*, "If there was a corner that can be cut, we do it. We're driving a thousand-dollar car, we rent this place. ... I clean with vinegar instead of getting a fancy product...It's absolutely horrifying to go from something to really nothing...then have to start all over, change all of your plans, your entire life...We understood that there was a risk but we didn't think that the company was just going to go under...It felt like robbery. It felt like a violation."[28]

As for the violator, in April 2008, the board of WaMu jettisoned Killinger, finally acknowledging the disaster he had fashioned. But he left the company having made a fortune that will make it possible for him to never work another day in his life, unlike the thousands of people who lost their life savings and face a future of destitution because of his actions.

Yet another CEO who got rich while his bank—and its customers—burned in 2008 was G. Kennedy "Ken" Thompson of Wachovia. In an echo of the WaMu collapse, Thompson gambled the future of his institution on the quick-buck profiteering available in the sub-prime mortgage business. Perhaps the dumbest move made by Thompson was the $24 billion purchase of Golden West Financial—which specialized in the toxic "option ARM" mortgages that WaMu was also heavily involved in. Golden West typically mixed option ARM mortgages into securities that it used to then borrow even more money—a scheme built on the quicksand of the real estate bubble. Even more irresponsibly, 60 percent of Golden West's mortgage business came from California, where the bubble was at its worst.[29]

It came as no surprise then, when Wachovia's net income in the fourth quarter of 2007 plunged to $51 million—or three cents a share—from $2.3 billion and $1.20 a share a year earlier, with the company's revenue falling 17 percent to $7.2 billion. (The company's mortgage-related losses were an astounding $1.7 billion.) This was not a problem for Thompson, however; while the bank was tanking, he was raking it in, taking home $15,653,559 in compensation in 2007.[30] Overall, during his eight years at the company, he earned $53,934,221, including more than $48.3 million in stock, and a nice $4.7 million in pay to be shelled out after he left the company.

And his departure was soon to come. In June 2008, Thompson was forced out of Wachovia after the bank had seen its stock nose dive by 40 percent and announced its first quarterly loss in seven years, slashing its dividend by 41 percent just a month after posting a first-quarter loss of $708 million, 80 percent higher than the number the bank had initially reported. Thompson, though, walked away from the rumble a very rich man.

And the story doesn't end there, as the legacy of Thompson's mismanagement lives on, and may yet drag down another big bank. With Wachovia struggling to stay solvent, Wells Fargo swooped in to purchase the bank (after a nasty tussle for control with Citigroup—which would have its own massive financial problems) for $15 billion in stock. But, as of the beginning of 2009, Wells Fargo was struggling to clean up Wachovia's gargantuan toxic mess: a $122 billion option ARM portfolio. Wells Fargo agreed to write off about one-third of that portfolio, but that may not be enough, according to analysts.[31]

"We are not going to be a bunch of crazy, anti-business liberals"

A final, yet crucial point that must be emphasized is how our political leaders conspired to sow the seeds of the looting that lead to the catastrophic financial collapse of 2008. And this cannot be viewed through the lens of partisanship—by partisan meaning "Democrat" versus "Republican." As I pointed out earlier in the book, while the Republican Party has certainly earned the right to wear the badge of defender of the "Free Market," Democrats have been no less tolerant of the mindless, greedy scheming atmosphere that has pervaded the real estate and financial sectors over the past several years.

For example, the top recipients of the $1.3 million in campaign contributions from Angelo Mozilo's Countrywide Financial since 1989 have been both Republicans and Democrats, with about $265,000 flowing to candidates in 2008 alone—when the crisis was already underway and therefore well-known to politicians. You can see the bipartisan nature of Countrywide's largesse just by looking at this list of some of the top financial recipients of the company's money from 1989 through 2008:

Republicans
Rep. Ed Royce (CA)—$37,500
Rep. Spencer Bachus (AL)—$22,000
Rep. Pete Sessions (TX)—$18,750
Rep. Elton Gallegly (CA)—$14,550

Rep. David Dreier (CA)—$12,500
Rep. Tom Feeney (FL)—$11,000
Sen. John McCain (AZ)—$9,950

Democrats
Rep. Paul E. Kanjorski (PA)—$24,250
Sen. Barack Obama (IL)—$22,900
Sen. Christopher J. Dodd (CT)—$20,000
Rep. Brad Sherman (CA)—$19,500
Sen. Tim Johnson (SD)—$17,000
Rep. Joseph Crowley (NY)—$14,500
Sen. Hillary Clinton (NY)—$14,400
Sen. John Kerry (MA)—$12,080
Sen. Dianne Feinstein (CA)—$12,000
Rep. Barney Frank (MA)—$11,000[32]

When the government put together the corporate welfare bailout fund contained in the Troubled Assets Relief Program (TARP), the same "bipartisan" game was played, as the 161 companies eligible for TARP money divvied up their political action money pretty much evenly among the parties, handing out a slightly bigger share—51 percent—to Republicans, though individual donors from the companies favored Democrats with 61 percent of their contributions. And those influence peddlers knew exactly where to target their money. "Some of the top recipients of contributions from companies receiving TARP money are the same members of Congress who chair committees charged with regulating the financial sector and overseeing the effectiveness of this unprecedented government program," reported The Center for Responsive Politics in February 2009. The list of recipients included Senator Chris Dodd of Connecticut, chairman of the Senate Committee on Banking, Housing and Urban Affairs, who received $854,200 from TARP companies during the 2008 election cycle, and Senator Max Baucus of Montana, chair of the Senate Finance Committee, who received $279,000. In total, "members of the Senate Committee on Banking, Housing and Urban Affairs, Senate Finance Committee and House Financial Services Committee received $5.2 million from TARP recipients in the 2007-2008 election cycle. President Obama collected at least $4.3 million from employees at these companies for his presidential campaign."[33]

When it comes to the connection between Democratic Party politics and the financial industry, Exhibit A is Senator Charles Schumer of New York. As a hyper-focused party builder, Schumer is very good at his job; during his tenure as head of the Democratic Senatorial Campaign Committee, the party picked up fifteen seats, going from a 43-member minority in 2006 to a 58-seat majority in 2008 (two independents—Bernie Sanders and Joseph Lieberman—caucus with the Democrats, bring the total Democratic number to 60).

To accomplish his goal of getting more Democrats elected—and as he sees it, to protect the interests of New York State—Schumer is an assiduous guardian of the interests of Wall Street. As *The New York Times* noted, "He has long been a pro-business Democrat and a fund-raising machine for the party, as well as a vociferous supporter of Wall Street issues in Washington, much the way Michigan lawmakers defend the auto industry and Iowa politicians work on behalf of corn farmers."[34] At a breakfast fundraiser held by the titans of Wall Street in September 2008, just as the financial crisis was upending the lives of millions of Americans, Schumer reassured his audience. "'We are not going to be a bunch of crazy, anti-business liberals,' one executive said, summarizing Mr. Schumer's remarks. 'We are going to be effective, moderate advocates for sound economic policies, good responsible stewards you can trust.'"[35]

Unfortunately, Schumer's trustworthy economic stewardship seems to extend only to his constituents on Wall Street, and not to the citizens he has been elected to serve. "He is serving the parochial interest of a very small group of financial people, bankers, investment bankers, fund managers, private equity firms, rather than serving the general public," said John C. Bogle, the founder and former chairman of the Vanguard Group, the giant mutual fund house. "It has hurt the American investor first and the average American tax-payer."[36] Schumer has been most protective of the private equity and hedge fund moguls—with the latter having played a major role in the upheaval of the financial system with its huge bets on mortgage-related securities and its pursuit of gigantic profits generated in large part by the launching of destabilizing corporate takeovers that were financed by massive amounts of new debt.

Schumer's protection of the hedge fund industry came to the forefront in 2007 after a furor erupted in the wake of several stories detailing the miniscule amount hedge fund managers were paying in taxes on their obscene earnings. Rather than being taxed at the top rate of 35 percent, the hedge fund managers were only paying 15 percent through a loophole called "carried interest." To understand carried interest, you have to first understand how money managers get paid in the rarified world of private equity. First, they receive a fee, which is a percentage of the funds they invest. This fee is usu-ally in the range of two percent, and is taxed like your run-of-the-mill wage income. Second, and far more lucratively, money manag-ers get a fee based on the performance of their fund—a fee in the range of 20 percent. It's the second fee that is the so-called "carried interest"—and it's how the money managers of private equity funds underwrite their Piccassos, yachts and mansions.

In the normal world of taxable income (and let me say that noth-ing in the tax code is simple when it comes to schemes that allow the audacity of greed to flourish), carried interest "is a right to receive a specified share (often 20 percent) of the profits ultimately earned by an investment fund without contributing a corresponding share of the fund's financial capital. It is part of the standard compensation package for managers of private equity funds."[37] The "carried inter-est" is taxed as investment income—at the capital gains level of 15 percent (much lower than the top wage income rate), even though most of these managers invest very little, if any, of their own money.

To understand the mammoth influence of "carried interest" on the looting of America, you need to grasp these facts: private equity and hedge funds collectively have more than $2 trillion under management (based on 2007 figures), with the private equity market alone having skyrocketed from about $5 billion in 1980 to more than $1 trillion today. In 2006 alone, private equity firms raised over $240 billion in capital—an astonishing figure. And, even more astonishing is the concentration of the business in a few hands, with the five largest firms raising an average of $30 billion each.[38]

Consider the practical effect of carried interest: a private equity honcho hauling down millions of dollars in "incentive" is taxed at a 15 percent rate, while the receptionist who works in his office, or the police officer who guards the equity baron's property, probably earn $50,000 or so if they're lucky—and pay a 25 percent tax rate on that income (not to mention payroll taxes), a far larger share of their income than the fellow who banks "carried interest."

When this all came to light in 2007, it struck some people as patently unfair. In June of that year, Representative Sander Levin, Democrat of Michigan, introduced a bill to correct the loophole that was depriving the government of billions of dollars in tax revenue. In pushing for the change, Levin said, "Congress must ensure that our tax code is fair. We have to be sure that the lower capital gains tax rate is not being inappropriately substituted for the tax rate on wages and earnings. Investment fund employees should not pay a lower rate of tax on their compensation for services than other Americans. These investment managers are being paid to provide a service to their limited partners and fairness requires they be taxed at the rates applicable to service income just as any other American worker."[39]

In response, the members of the elite howled in protest. The U.S. Chamber of Commerce set up a website to attack the proposed changes, and issued a report with the ominous headline, "Chamber Study Shows Tax Increases on Partnerships Pose A Great Risk to the U.S. Economy."[40] In February 2007, the industry set up its own "advocacy, communications and research organization" (read: lobbying group) called the Private Equity Council.[41] During the 2008 election cycle, the private equity industry donated $22.5 million—almost four times the amount it had shelled out during the previous cycle—with 58 percent of that money aimed at influencing the Democrats who controlled Congress.[42] During the same election cycle, the hedge fund industry donated $16.5 million—almost four times what it had donated in the previous election cycle—with 65 percent of that money going to Democrats.[43] The end result of this private equity and hedge fund money? "Lobbyists for a handful of super-rich private equity and hedge fund managers are working hard on Capitol Hill to block the House bill from advancing in the Senate," reported *Reuters* in November 2007.[44]

As pressure mounted to fix the inequity, Schumer rode to the rescue—using his position as the third-ranking Democrat in the Senate and his seats on both the Banking and Finance committees to block any attempt to raise the tax on carried interest to 35 percent. In doing so, he deprived the federal government of billions of dollars in revenue that could have been used for health care, roads, schools and other social needs. "The United States and New York City must remain the leading country and city in the world for financial services and capital formation," Schumer said at the time, "and we shouldn't do anything to jeopardize that position and make it easier for capital and ideas to flow to London or anywhere else."[45] Not coincidentally, in the first six months of 2007, when the controversy erupted, Schumer's Democratic Senate campaign committee raised at least $2 million from private equity and hedge fund interests.[46] The upshot of all this: as of 2009, nothing has been done to correct the inequity, and "carried interest," and the legalized robbery it allows, lives on. And the chances of substantial change happening remain relatively small: When he was a member of Congress, White House Chief of Staff Rahm Emanuel was the top recipient in the House of money from hedge funds, private equity firms and the larger securities/investment industry in 2008; overall, during his six years in the House, he received more contributions from individuals and PACs in the securities and investment business than from any other industry.[47]

The populist outrage that has coursed through the American public since the economic catastrophe of 2008 has elicited a whole host of rhetorical promises from politicians to change the culture of Washington. But, almost a year later, have our politicians changed the way they do business? The answer, sadly, is for the most part, no. And, so, you have to wonder: can we do anything to change the political and economic system so that we can find our way out of the current financial crisis, and not face another one like it in the future?

Conclusion: A Return To Sanity

When Barack Obama was sworn into office on January 20, 2009, he stood on the steps of the Capitol, and, speaking to nearly two million people spread out on the Mall, as well as tens of millions more watching on television (and the internet) and listening on the radio around the country and across the globe, said:

> Our economy is badly weakened, a consequence of greed and irresponsibility on the part of some, but also our collective failure to make hard choices and prepare the nation for a new age...

> ...Nor is the question before us whether the market is a force for good or ill. Its power to generate wealth and expand freedom is unmatched, but this crisis has reminded us that without a watchful eye, the market can spin out of control—and that a nation cannot prosper long when it favors only the prosperous...

> ...What is required of us now is a new era of responsibility—a recognition, on the part of every American, that we have duties to ourselves, our nation, and the world, duties that we do not grudgingly accept but rather seize gladly, firm in the knowledge that there is nothing so satisfying to

the spirit, so defining of our character, than giving our all to a difficult task...

Obama was certainly correct in skewing the greed and irresponsibility on "the part of some," but he unfortunately got the rest of it all wrong. First off, his speaking about the "collective failure to make hard choices," implied that millions of average Americans had acted recklessly and fueled the economic crisis that was facing the country. In reality, except for the small, greedy elite that we have discussed throughout this book, most Americans have in fact been making "hard" choices each and every day for the past several years.

Choices about what bills to pay and what bills to put off because their paychecks were too small to make ends meet.

Choices about whether or not to take on another minimum-wage part-time job so that they could put food on the table for their families—even if taking that extra job meant fewer hours of sleep per night or less time spent with their children.

Choices about whether to raid their small nest eggs—money carefully saved up over years—to pay for surgery or a health care emergency, or to just make sure there was enough gas in the car so they could get to work.

The truth is that the overwhelming majority of people in cities and towns across the nation have acted quite responsibly given an economic system that has, for the past quarter century, increasingly denied them the fruits of their hard work while shoveling the vast wealth they have created into the hands of a self-selected few.

Ultimately, if "change" is the buzzword of this American moment, we can only move forward toward real change if we are willing to first address the prime culprit for our current troubles—namely, the culture of free market ideology and corporate greed that has enslaved this country for nearly three decades. And, even if we focus our attention where it rightfully belongs, the battle to change this country will not be easy, as those in power have a powerful posse at their side—politicians, media talking heads, financial analysts—all ready to justify the necessity of the "free" market, no matter its costs to regular Americans. We must understand that the elite is not going to give up its exalted status—ordering up their private jets at a moment's notice to fly off to their chalets where they can dine on the finest foods and drink $1,000 bottles of wine—without a fight.

However, before we go to war, we must first identify the specific battles we need to fight in order to create change we can all believe in. Toward that end, what follows are seven proposals that we can use as a blueprint for establishing economic fairness for ordinary Americans while at the same time putting a halt to the culture of greed that has infected our country. The battle against entrenched corporate and political interests is going to be long and difficult, but hopefully these proposals can act as a guide to help us restore some semblance of sanity to our economy gone wild.

The Shame of the Minimum Wage

Proposal #1: Immediately raise the minimum wage to $10 an hour, with additional increases over the next five years until it reaches $20 an hour, which would begin to return some level of justice to working America.

While we should be happy for those who have received increases in their gross pay because of the minimum wage hikes in 2008 and 2009, we should keep in mind that, at the grand new sum of $7.25 an hour, the current minimum wage remains a sad commentary on the state of our social safety net, our economy and our political system.

As we saw earlier in the book, the minimum wage math is pretty stark. If someone worked 40 hours a week, 52 weeks a year at the current rate, they would earn $15,080—assuming they didn't take a single vacation or sick day, and received no pension. And, taking into account the cost of food, housing, gas, clothing and the other necessities of life, $15,080 per year is certainly not enough to keep most people out of poverty. My friend David Morris, a brilliant thinker who runs the Institute for Local Self-Reliance, said—with his usual sarcasm—of those who work for the minimum wage in this country: "well, at least they're better off than a poor Nigerian."

Even if President Obama keeps the promise he made during his campaign to raise the minimum wage to $9.50 by 2011, a person earning that amount would still make under $20,000 a year ($19,760).[1] And, two years from now, that sum will certainly buy even less than it does today, if the rising costs of housing, food and gasoline are any guide—putting that sum barely, if at all, above the federal poverty rate. It is, therefore, false and misleading for the president to describe his proposal as a "living wage." It should rather be described, at best, as a "barely keeping out of bankruptcy" wage.

Part of the problem is that there is a compact between our government and the private sector which accepts vast poverty as a matter of economic policy. For example, once upon a time, if you worked hard and were productive, that translated directly into your paycheck. Not anymore. From 2000 to roughly 2007, productivity went up 20 percent—while the median hourly wage went up only 3 percent. As I mentioned earlier in the book, taking into account productivity, the minimum wage today should be $19.12—nearly three times what it actually is. At that level, you would make almost $40,000 a year—not an outstanding amount given today's high cost of living and the likelihood that you would not have a job with health care and a pension, but at least in the realm of an above bankruptcy income level.

Unfortunately, market fundamentalism enforces poverty as a way of life for too many American workers, as something society must accept so that the economy can grow (read: CEOs can get rich). President Obama's minimum wage proposal reinforces the acceptance of the market fundamentalists' view of poverty. Simply put, poverty cannot end in America until the precepts of market fundamentalism are rejected.

"Medicare For All—Now!"

Proposal #2: Pass H.R. 676, the so-called "Medicare for All Now" bill, in order to enact single-payer health care.[2]

Aside from the moral issue of covering every single American and making health care a right, not a privilege, the passage of H.R. 676 would also save the economy hundreds of billions of dollars and immediately make American-based businesses competitive around the world with companies that operate out of countries that provide national health care to their citizens.

Currently, one of the greatest looters of this country is the private insurance industry, which rips off billions of dollars from the pockets of regular people and from small and medium-sized businesses. Looking at our health care system, you can see how market fundamentalism literally ends up killing people.

During the 2008 Democratic presidential primary battle, Senator Hillary Clinton made much of what she said were the scars that she had "earned" during the health care fight of the early 1990s. The implication was that the former First Lady had fought for health care reform and in *losing*, was battle-tested and far more ready to take on the upcoming health care battle than her opponent. But the problem was that Clinton learned the wrong lesson from her experiences in the 1990s—and President Obama is poised to repeat the same mistake.

The lesson from the 1990s battle is simple: **a health care plan that covers every person at an affordable cost cannot be negotiated with the private insurance industry and cannot be run on a for-profit basis**. As long as health care is considered a profit-making business, "universal health care" will not be universal, or affordable. Simply put, health care cannot be left to the designs of the free market. Even though the private insurance industry is bloated with administrative inefficiency (partly because of the obscene salaries paid to insurance company CEOs), market fundamentalism will always choose the insatiable drive for higher profits over proper, affordable care for people.

According to Physicians For A National Health Plan (www. pnhp.org), under a single-payer system, "all Americans would be covered for all medically necessary services, including: doctor, hospital, long-term care, mental health, dental, vision, prescription drug and medical supply costs. Patients would regain free choice of doctor and hospital, and doctors would regain autonomy over patient care." For doctors, single-payer would mean that they would be paid "according to a negotiated formulary or receive salary from a hospital or nonprofit HMO / group practice." In addition, hospitals would receive a budget for operating expenses, and "expensive equipment purchases would be managed by regional health planning boards." "Modest" new taxes would replace premiums and out-of-pocket payments currently paid by individuals and business, while costs would be "controlled through negotiated fees, global budgeting and bulk purchasing."

In terms of financing, a single-payer system would be funded "by eliminating private insurers and recapturing their administrative waste." Under the present system, private insurance companies spend tons of money on things that have nothing to do with health care, including "overhead, underwriting, billing, sales and marketing departments as well as huge profits and exorbitant executive pay." These needless administration costs eat up 31 percent of health dollars in this country. The way to recapture this wasted money is through single-payer financing. Ultimately, a single payer system would save more than $350 billion per year, "enough to provide comprehensive coverage to everyone without paying any more than we already do."[3]

A Stable and Secure Retirement

Proposal #3: Create a national guaranteed universal pension plan, backed by the government, so that people can be sure that their retirement years will not be threatened by the wild swings of Wall Street.

It should be probably pretty clear by now, especially after you have read about the great fortunes of CEOs like Edward Whitacre, that while executives have been socking away massive piles of cash for their retirement years over the past decade, the people who worked for them haven't been as fortunate. As a worker in the United States, it used to be the case that you could look into the future and expect to enjoy a decent retirement, the result of the "three-legged stool" of Social Security, a defined-benefit pension and personal savings.

For most people today, at least two of the legs of that stool have been sawed off. While Social Security is still there (and, despite the fear-mongering, quite solvent for many years to come), raise your hand if you have a defined-benefit pension (less than 20 percent of workers now have such a plan). And how's your 401(k) done lately?

In the same way that we need a universal health care plan in this country, we also need a government-sponsored universal pension plan. In his proposal for "Universal Voluntary Accounts," the economist Dean Bakers shows why a government-backed plan (UVA) is superior to the run-of-the-mill defined contribution (DC) plan that many for-profit financial service firms try to sell workers: "If a worker contributes $1,000 annually to a DC plan with an annual fee of 1.5 percent, she will have accumulated $54,900 toward retirement after 35 years. By contrast, if the same worker contributes $1,000 annually for 35 years to a UVA system with a fee of 0.3 percent annually, she will have accumulated $69,400, or 26 percent more." In addition, Baker writes that by simply eliminating waste in the current system, we can "easily add 30 to 35 percent to the money that workers have available in retirement."[4]

The beauty of the UVA plan is that workers can create their own defined-benefit option so that they can count on receiving a specific amount of money each month, rather than worrying about the swings of the stock market. As Baker explains:

> For example, a worker putting aside $1,000 annually for 35 years (as described earlier) would be able to get a retirement annuity of $6,600 a year at age 65 using the same conserva- tive assumptions as in the earlier calculation. If she waited until age 67 to begin collecting, the annuity would rise to almost $8,000 a year. In the case where a low-income work-

er received a government subsidy of $300 annually for 35 years, he would be able to get a retirement annuity of almost $2,000 a year at age 65 and almost $2,400 a year at age 67. Again, these are not large sums, but the median income for a household over age 65 is currently just $26,000 and more than a third of older households have an annual income of less than $18,000. Increasing the income of retirees at or below the median by $2,000-$2,400 per year would likely make a substantial difference in their standard of living.

The defined-benefit option in the UVA system works in the same manner as defined-benefit pension plans do in the private sector, by removing market risk for workers, which is then assumed by financial institutions or the government. "In principle," Baker concludes, "a large long-lived entity like a state government can assume market risk because it will survive through up and down markets."[5]

Get Real About Taxes

Proposal #4: Repeal the Bush tax cuts, and raise the top income tax rates—at a minimum—to 40 percent and 45 percent, and add a new 50 percent income tax bracket for those with taxable income over $1 million. In addition, tax investment income as ordinary income.

Until we stop the moronic rhetoric that says that every economic ill can be addressed by cutting taxes, our political debate will be stuck in an ideological straightjacket. The truth is that the tax cut discussion is a distraction from the far more important challenges facing American workers—as well as an unnecessary drain on the U.S. Treasury. Tossing workers a few hundred extra bucks hobbles the government's ability to do its job, and also undercuts our ability to launch national health care, fund infrastructure projects and move the economy towards a carbon-free future.

We actually have plenty of money sloshing around the country to do the right things—if we demand that the wealthy pay their fair share. If that happened, with very little trouble, we could generate another $350 billion per year to fulfill society's needs—and that money would come from the top five percent of income owners, and, mostly, from the top one percent.

In 2008, with the help of Citizens For Tax Justice (www.ctj.org), the premier non-partisan organization focusing exclusively on tax issues, I put together an alternative tax structure which would raise the top income tax rates to 40 percent and 45 percent (the top rate is now 35 percent for married taxable income above $351,000), add a top rate of 50 percent for those with taxable income higher than $1 million and—this is crucial—tax investment income as ordinary income (this proposal assumes that Congress will eventually fix the Alternative Minimum Tax).

Patch the AMT, raise the top two income tax rates to 40% and 45%, add a new 50% income tax bracket for those with taxable income over $1 million, tax investment income as ordinary income.

	% share of tax cut	% share of tax cut	% with tax hike	% share of tax hike	average tax change	Total change ($-bill)
Lowest 20%	—	—	2.1%	0.0%	$+3	$ +0.1
Second 20%	—	—	6.9%	0.2%	+14	+0.4
Middle 20%	3.2%	0.9%	13.4%	0.4%	+18	+0.5
Fourth 20%	26.6%	12.8%	23.8%	1.5%	-170	−4.9
Next 10%	68.4%	28.4%	19.7%	1.4%	-1,131	−16.2
Next 5%	79.0%	25.5%	17.7%	1.2%	-2,040	−14.6
Next 4%	72.2%	32.0%	26.6%	4.2%	-1,866	−10.7
Next 1%	5.1%	0.4%	93.8%	91.2%	+179,095	+256.4
ALL	19.4%	100.0%	13.9%	100.0%	$ +1,454	+211.1

This plan would help the country realize an additional $211 billion in annual net revenues, with 91 percent of those revenues coming from the richest one percent of Americans (the above model should be adjusted to eliminate tax reductions for higher income earners). Another $150 billion per year would come from a very tiny "thank you for playing" fee of 0.25 percent on Wall Street stock transactions, an amount so miniscule that the small investor wouldn't even notice it. However, the lion's share of income would come from the big traders and speculators who move millions of shares a day in an attempt to jump on any gyration in the market. These traders benefit from numerous government protections, not the least of which is a regulatory system that is supposed to prevent, *in theory*, fraud and crazy speculation. Perhaps such a tax would help these people exercise some restraint, preventing some of the wild trading made based mostly on rumors by those thirsting for a quick buck.

My main intention for this plan, though, is shared responsibility: If you want to live—and in the cases of the corporate elite, thrive—in this society, you must make a contribution to its well-being. However, in the current climate, increasing the tax rates for the richest people in society is *not* an economic challenge; it is instead, a political challenge. There is, for example, no credible evidence that shows that higher tax rates—at least, of the amount suggested in my plan—will have a negative effect on our economy. In fact, the opposite is true: taxing the richest individuals in the country will be a boon to all citizens if we give that revenue back to the government in order to help it create a national health care plan, which will reduce the burden on individuals and businesses; invest in a massive infrastructure program which will create millions of new jobs; and inject a large amount of new capital into the economy to provide a huge boost in earning power for individuals.

Frankly, my alternative tax plan is a relatively modest proposal. We could—and should—raise the top tax rates even higher, with the top rate for the richest 1 percent set at least 50 percent. As a basis of comparison, from 1951 to 1964, the post-war era that America's leaders and pundits like to point to as the beginning of the great economic upswing in this country, the top rate was 91 percent for married couples making $200,000 and up.

Bring Back the Power of Unions

Proposal #5: Pass the Employee Free Choice Act. The single most important step we can take to rebalance the levels of power in our economy is to increase unionization. If you want me to give an entirely predictable and moralizing speech about why every worker should join a union, I can do that—and I would believe it too. Simply put, no democracy can survive without a strong labor movement that acts as a bulwark for employee rights in the workplace. But I'll save your grey cells here and jump quickly to this thought: unions are good for business, the corporate bottom line and America's prosperity.

The logic is simple. The severe recession and the economic turmoil we are currently facing are, at heart, the end result of a three-decade long wage depression. Without any real increase in wages since the 1970s, consumers have piled up debt, with Americans overall credit card debt growing from $211 billion in 1989 to $971 billion in 2009.[6] (That comes out to $3,184 per person and $8,299 per household). With their credit cards maxed out, many Americans have had no choice but to turn to their sole remaining economic lifeline: home equity. It is estimated that homeowners sucked out $1.2 trillion in home equity from 2002 through 2007, not to pay for mansions and yachts, but for basic living expenses.[7]

With credit dried up, how will future consumer spending—which accounts for 70 percent of our economic engine—be financed? We are now facing years, or maybe even a decade, in which consumers will have to go through a painful unwinding of the debt morass they have sunken into—not because they were profligate but because they had no other options. For thirty years, most people's paychecks have been shrinking, and now they simply have no money left—as the recent steep decline in consumer spending proved.

What does this have to do with unions? Basic math: wages for union members are higher than wages for non-union members. According to the Center for American Progress, "Over the four-year period between 2004 and 2007, unionized workers' wages were on average 11.3 percent higher than non-union workers with similar characteristics. That means that, all else equal, American workers that join a union will earn 11.3 percent more—or $2.26 more per hour in 2008 dollars—than their otherwise identical non-union counterparts."[8] In addition, union members typically enjoy better pensions and health care than non-union members, as union workers are "28.2 percent more likely to be covered by employer-provided health insurance and 53.9 percent more likely to have employer-provided pensions."[9] Higher wages of course mean that people have more money to spend, which is a boon for the economy. In the short-term, the knee jerk corporate practice of opposing unions might leave a few more shekels for the bottom line—partly to finance gargantuan pay, bonuses and pensions for a few executives—but, in the long-term, it is a practice that is actually bad for business, as it hurts consumers' ability to buy the products that businesses produce.

To increase union membership—and therefore increase consumer buying power—it is necessary that we pass the Employee Free Choice Act. EFCA would, among other things, make it easier for workers to join a union by declaring that a union is automatically formed if a majority of employees at a company sign cards saying they want to join one (the so-called "card check" option"), increase penalties for companies that violate employee rights and assist workers in reaching their first union contract.

As the contentious battle over ECFA has been fought over the past few years, the business community has had two choices: It could continue to hang on to its ideological opposition to unions, and trot out the fear-mongering rhetoric that unionization means saddling consumers with higher prices, in the process spending billions of dollars to fight union organizing drives, create a war-like atmosphere in the workplace and economically, keep workers (meaning, consumers) from opening up their pocketbooks and buying the products companies sell.

Or in the privacy of their offices, business leaders could have been dispassionately non-ideological and done a little back of the envelope calculation. Yes, having to deal with a union might mean sacrificing a little control and power, and upper management would have to deal with having a watchdog looking over its shoulder. And yes, executives would have to let go of some of their large pay and benefits. In exchange, however, a more broadly shared prosperity between workers and employers would mean a stronger corporate bottom line, as workers who make more money will buy more cars, electronics, clothes, food and other goods and products. At the end of the day, being pro-union might even make business leaders feel good, not just because they increased profits, but because they also opened the door to a slightly better life for their fellow citizens.

Unfortunately, the anti-union mindset has clearly won out when it comes to the EFCA. "It will be a boot on the throat of business and it will compound exponentially the economic difficulties that American businesses are suffering today," said Mark McKinnon, a spokesman for the anti-EFCA group the Workforce Fairness Institute.[10] Home Depot co-founder Bernard Marcus added that EFCA was a "planned hostile takeover" of company's human resource departments, and that the legislation "eviscerates traditional democratic principles."[11] Sadly, as this book went to press, it appeared that the Employee Free Choice Act was, for the moment, dead in Congress—mainly because of the opposition of the business community.

Ending the Legalized Corruption of Our Electoral System

Proposal #6—Publicly-financed elections. If we want to weaken the power of "The Club" to make the rules that grease CEO greed, we have to first end the legalized corruption of our electoral system, which allows huge amounts of money from corporate interests to buy politicians from both major political parties. The only way to do that is to have publicly-financed elections.

It has been said that President Obama's election showed the power of small money donations—primarily raised via the internet—and suggested the waning power of big money. There is no doubt that internet fundraising—and, in particular, the Obama campaign's online prowess, which obliterated what was previously thought to be an impregnable political fortress (the Clinton machine)—created some space for the "average voter" to weigh in with his or her financial contribution. But the truth is that one-third of the staggering amount of money that Obama raised through August 2008 (and that number certainly rose in the final months of the election), came from donations of $1,000 or more. Much of that money was raised by Obama "bundlers," who raised amounts over $50,000 (a few raised six figure amounts) for the campaign. And not surprisingly, many of those bundlers came "from industries with critical interests in Washington," mainly law, securities and investments, real estate and entertainment.[12] In addition, at least 100 Obama bundlers were "top executives or brokers from investment businesses: nearly two dozen work[ed] for financial titans like Lehman Brothers, Goldman Sachs or Citigroup." The need for massive amounts of money to finance elections creates an unhealthy mix between politicians and the business community.

Despite the temptation, we shouldn't pile on Barack Obama, as he was simply playing within the rules of a system he didn't create. What we need to do is trash our corrupt election system and replace it with one that allows the public's voice to be heard over the money of the elite. The only way to do this is with publicly-financed elections.

Introduced after the scandal of Watergate, the public financing of elections was initially quite successful. In 1986, ten years after the first publicly-financed presidential election, a bipartisan commission headed by Robert Strauss, a former head of the Democratic Party, and Melvin R. Laird, the Secretary of Defense under President Richard Nixon, declared that, "Public financing of presidential elections has clearly proved its worth in opening up the process, reducing the influence of individuals and groups, and virtually ending corruption in presidential election finance."[13] Fast forward a couple of decades, and recent presidential elections have made a mockery of the publicly financed system. In 2004, both George W. Bush and John Kerry opted out of public financing, as did both Democratic candidates, Hillary Clinton and Barack Obama, in 2008. The 2008 Republican nominee John McCain only opted into the system because he was having difficulty raised money from private sources.

Until we fix this system, politicians—even if they actually want to do the work of the people—will have no choice but to spend most of their time soliciting money from wealthy elites, who in turn will expect politicians to do their bidding once they get in office. According to Common Cause, publicly-financed or "clean" elections would sever "the direct link between campaign donations and political favors, ensuring that politicians are accountable to the public interest rather than special interests"; give voters "the opportunity to make a decision based on the merits of the candidates rather than their fundraising abilities"; and "allow candidates, and officeholders seeking reelection, to spend less time dialing-for-dollars and more time focusing on solving the pressing challenges confronting our nation."[14]

As Theodore Roosevelt presciently said back in 1907, "The need for collecting large campaign funds would vanish if Congress provided an appropriation for the proper and legitimate expenses of each of the great national parties."[15]

"The Most Profoundly Anti-American Thing I have Ever Seen"

Proposal #7: We need to push for changes that impose a proportional pay cut on executives equal to whatever pay cuts their workers are forced to take—and I would add that, given the level of pensions granted executives, it should not be a one to one ratio, but one that significantly scales back executive pensions in comparison to rank and file workers.

I'm sick and tired of reading about companies that file for bankruptcy so that they can tear up union contracts and terminate pensions—while continuing to give their executives hundreds of millions of dollars in compensation. You couldn't find a better contrast to illustrate this immoral monstrosity than how our economic elites treated the now infamous executives at AIG versus the posture taken toward members of the United Auto Workers.

The AIG story may have faded from memory a bit, but recall that the company got itself into a financial hellhole because of extraordinary mismanagement by a handful of executives and high-level traders who effectively bankrupted the company by handcuffing it with $2.7 trillion in trades that went sour, bad trades that the taxpayers had to ultimately foot the bill for. In just six months' time—from September 2008 to March 2009—the federal government handed out $173.3 billion in federal aid to AIG, turning the government—that would actually be you and me—into the company's majority owner, with a nearly 80 percent stake.

However, did the failed executives at AIG suffer for their incompetence? Yes, if you consider suffering to be the $165 million in "retention" bonuses they were given—some of which went to people who had already left the company. When a public furor erupted, we were told that the bonuses still had to be paid because the contracts the company signed with the executives were somehow sacrosanct, untouchable and binding unless one could prove illegal behavior (as opposed to simply legal incompetence and malfeasance).

The point is this: while the government did not push AIG to file for bankruptcy, the company was effectively bankrupt. But, no executive was asked to take a financial hit—at least until a public outcry erupted across the nation, triggering an attempt by Congress to slap a 90 percent tax on bonuses for traders, executives and bankers at AIG earning more than $250,000 per year.[16] (Ultimately, about $50 million worth of the bonus money was returned). However, the executives at AIG who gave back their money did so not because they believed they had done anything wrong, but simply because they had been pressured to do so. In fact, the March 21, 2009 edition of *The Financial Times* carried a front-page story quoting these poor bankers decrying the public outcry over their bonuses as a "McCarthy witch-hunt" and the "most profoundly anti-American thing I have ever seen."[17]

During the same time period as the AIG crisis, the Big Three auto companies were on the verge of collapse because of a colossal failure by management to design cars that were fuel-efficient, sky-rocketing oil prices during the summer of 2008 and the global economic meltdown, which shattered car sales. Trooping to Capitol Hill in December of 2008, the auto executives put out a tin cup, asking for a pittance—$38 billion in total—to save their companies, and the tens of thousands of good-paying jobs, and decent retirement benefits, that had been won over the course of several generations by the United Auto Workers (not to mention another half-million jobs at auto suppliers who produce parts for the Big Three). Compared to the hundreds of billions of dollars shoveled out to financial institutions, the auto companies were asking for chump change.

And the contracts of the auto workers? Were they sacrosanct and protected, as the AIG bonuses were? Did the talking heads on television, the columnists in newspapers and the politicians in government stand up and scream, "don't touch those contracts—they were negotiated before this crisis and those workers should not be asked to give back money, especially since they had nothing to do with the mismanagement of their companies"? Of course not. Even after a series of painful concessions made by rank and file workers over a number of years (including lowering starting pay and cutting benefits) to try to keep the companies afloat, from Capitol Hill to the screaming madmen on television, there were repeated cries to not give a dime to the auto companies, force them into bankruptcy and shred the UAW's contracts. For example, one month after losing the presidential election to Barack Obama, Senator John McCain said that auto makers needed to make changes in "salaries, wages and benefits." He added that if the automakers couldn't be forced into outright bankruptcy, they should undergo a "bankruptcy-like solution" that would reduce compensation levels for workers in order to make the automakers competitive with foreign manufacturers. [18]

It was about as clear a double-standard as one could want: in the "free market," the law apparently protected executives who looted their companies, but had nothing to offer the regular Joe or Jane who came to work every day and broke his or her back to earn a decent paycheck, in the process creating the very wealth that underwrote the lavish pay for top executives. If one picture told the whole story, during the testimony of the auto executives before Congress in December 2008, "a large chart stood just to the side of the dais titled, 'Taxpayer-Funded Bailouts.' With large blue bars, it showed $300 billion for Citigroup; $200 billion for the mortgage giants, Fannie Mae and Freddie Mac; $150 billion for the insurance conglomerate, American International Group; $29 billion for the failed investment bank, Bear Stearns. At the bottom of the chart were three more blue bars, each with a red question mark after them: $18 billion for General Motors; $13 billion for Ford; $7 billion for Chrysler."[19]

Perhaps if executives were forced to take the same pay cuts that they impose on their workers, maybe they—and "The Club" members who enable them— wouldn't be so cavalier about demanding that workers assume pay and benefit cuts to "save" the companies they work for.

Can We See A Different World?

While the seven proposals I have outlined represent an initial movement a more equitable economic system, they won't have a true impact if we don't take on the biggest obstacle standing in our way, which is reexamining the basic idea of the role and power of the corporation in America and around the globe and, by extension, the concept of the "free market." To make any kind of real and actual change in our current system, we need to rethink what a "healthy" economy means in a world where two billion people live on two dollars or less a day and all of us exist on a planet on the brink of environmental collapse.

In an essay I wrote in the mid-1990s titled "The Edifice Complex," I argued that we live in the culture of the "Boundless Bull," a term coined by Herman E. Daly, formerly a senior economist at the World Bank and now a Professor of Public Policy at the University of Maryland. Daly helped develop the concept of "unequal growth," which occurs when "increases in production come at an expense in resources and well-being that is worth more than the items made."[20] Daly, at one time a free trader, explained back in 1990 how the Merrill Lynch bull was the metaphor for the U.S. economy. Of course, he didn't mean it in the context in which we now think of Merrill Lynch, as a humiliated, broken firm that was sold off to Bank of America in 2008 because of the recklessness, greed and incompetence of its leaders. No, Daly saw something else back then:

"If you want to know what is wrong with the American economy it is not enough to go to graduate school, read books, and study statistical trends—you also have to watch TV. Not the Sunday morning talking-head shows or even documentaries, and especially not the network news, but the really serious stuff—the commercials...One such ad opens with a bull trotting along a beach. He is a very powerful animal—nothing is likely to stop him. And since the beach is empty as far as the eye can see, there is nothing that could even slow him down. A chorus in the background intones: 'to...know...no...boundaries...' The bull trots off into the sunset...Finally we see the bull silhouetted against a burgundy sunset, standing in solitary majesty atop a mesa overlooking a great empty southwestern desert..." The message is clear: Merrill Lynch wants to put you into an individualistic, macho, world without limits—the U.S. economy.

Daly went on to write about how the bull represented unlimited optimism (and rising stock prices), which was based on the vision of an "empty world where strong, solitary individuals have free reign" and sell you growth, which requires "empty space to grow into." The message was that "In a world with no boundaries the poor can get richer while the rich get richer even faster. Our politicians find the boundless bull cult irresistible."[21]

The reason our political leaders find the boundless bull so irresistible is because it represents the culture that they—and consequently all of us—have been socialized from birth to applaud and celebrate. In the quintessentially American view of the world, we endure every economic downturn by waiting breathlessly for expansion. Promising renewed growth is the bi-partisan cornerstone of every major national political campaign, most recently articulated by Barack Obama's pledge to "change" America by laying "a new foundation for growth."

Our problem, however, is that as a global society, there will be no room to grow if we continue to consume resources like a parasite and fail to look at how wealth is distributed throughout the world. The globe has too many people, more than a billion of whom, according to conservative estimates, are unemployed or chronically underemployed and living in conditions below basic sustainable levels. We won't be able to shake the economic problems currently gripping us until we shift our cultural appetite for endless, often unhealthy growth.

If we return for a moment to Herman Daly, we learn that our problem is that we fail to distinguish between a growing economy that gets bigger, versus a developing economy that gets better. "An economy can therefore develop without growing, or grow without developing...The advantage of defining growth in terms of change in physical scale of the economy is that it forces us to think about the effects of a change in scale and directs attention to the concept of an ecologically sustainable scale, or perhaps even of an optimal scale." Daly sums up his argument by saying that in this case, "the apt image for the U.S. economy…is not the boundless bull on the empty beach, but the proverbial bull in the china shop. The boundless bull is too big and clumsy relative to its delicate environment. Why must it keep growing when it is already destroying more than its extra mass is worth?" Daly believes it is because "we fail to distinguish growth from development" and "refuse to fight poverty by redistribution and sharing, or by controlling our own numbers, leaving 'economic' growth as the only acceptable cure for poverty. But once we are beyond the optimal scale and growth makes us poorer rather than richer, even that reason becomes absurd."

We are constantly told, by liberals and conservatives alike, that economic security—in other words, more growth—will always come when we work harder, become more highly-skilled or better educated to compete in the world economy. That is just foolish. We already work harder, almost to the breaking point, than ever before in history. What is happening then? In part, the political leadership in this country has never had the courage to challenge (or worse, they are willing enablers) of the insatiable corporate search for profits. This is no dark, secret conspiracy; it is laid out in the open every day in the pages of publications like *The Wall Street Journal* and *Business Week* as well as being all over the internet. The corporate elite is not, and has never been, shy about their goals and though they are not averse to patriotic cheerleading to get their way, they are, to some extent, far more honest than political leaders, presumably because they face neither the pressure of re-election nor, as we have seen throughout this book, any kind of restraints on their behavior. More than fifteen years ago, these leaders openly told the government that "in order to survive, they are taking actions they believe are not in the national interest, including selling off key U.S. assets and placing R&D facilities and advanced manufacturing plants abroad."[22]

But, we cannot hide behind corporate behavior as the only obstacle to trying to reverse the looting of America. And there is where the ultimate contradictions and challenges for workers in this country, and for the rest of the progressive movement, lie. On the one hand, we tell our citizens that we seek to revive the "American Dream" for them. "It's a dream that we can find a job with wages that support a family," said then-presidential candidate Barack Obama on January 29, 2008. "That we can have health care that's affordable for when we get sick. That we can retire with dignity and security." But at the same time, our professed desire for a country where workers earn a sustainable wage, labor in safe conditions and live in communities relatively free of environmental disasters has been largely vanquished by decades of declining wages, no health insurance for nearly fifty million people, and a stripping away of retirement benefits for most workers.

So, we are faced with a conundrum. Clearly we cannot simultaneously champion the cult of growth—with its emphasis on riches for the few—on the one hand, and the notion of labor rights, universal health care and fair wages on the other. At the very least, what I am arguing for is honesty. It may be that a world of equitable distribution of resources is an idealistic fantasy that is not feasible given the past one hundred—and in particular the last thirty—years of human history. But, then, we should at least admit that we cannot give up our old ways, so engrained in our culture as they are, and then do our best to at least help make things somewhat more bearable for most of the rest of the country and the world. In doing so, however, we must also acknowledge to ourselves that we are not willing to guarantee a hospitable world for our descendants.

Of course, a bolder path would be more desirable and visionary. What we need is a real public debate to redefine the American Dream, not just a few speeches from our elected officials. Rather than blind growth, we should demand economic policies that construct a sustainable, equitable global economy by redistributing wealth and reducing population. We should focus on charting a developing economy—one that gets better for everyone but doesn't necessarily get bigger. In the long term, this might mean a different—lower, in the conventional way of thinking—standard of living for Americans, but a better quality of living with greater job security. And, with millions of Americans out of work because of the current recession, there is no better time than now to radically alter our thinking.

The first salvo in a national debate could be aimed at the perception that our societal growth has been—at least before 2008—essentially on an upward trend as measured by the Gross National Product (GNP) or Gross Domestic Product (GDP). When the media gleefully reports to us that the GNP or GDP has risen, is this good or bad? What does it measure? Who benefits? We have been socialized to accept the GNP and GDP as neutral indicators, devoid of political judgments and values. But, indeed, they are astonishingly political numbers: they ignore the costs of pollution (in fact, pollution gets counted twice—once when waste is created during production and again when it generates economic activity aimed at cleaning up toxic dumps or the air); income distribution (you can have a net rise in either indicator if the rich are getting richer even when the poor are sinking deeper into despair); and long-term resource depletion.

One alternative measure is dubbed the GPI: Genuine Progress Indicator.[23] Unlike the GDP/GNP standard, the GPI takes into account things such as resource depletion (the loss of resources we cannot replenish); unemployment and underemployment (as negative costs per hour); long-term environmental damage; income distribution; and the lifespan of consumer durables and public infrastructure. Once you use these measurements, a startlingly different picture emerges: GDP has been an illusion and has measured a life where the costs of production have not given us the benefits of a better life.

And the fact is we can reduce the cost of living in significant ways that help the general welfare. As Joel Rogers has observed,

Cities have natural economic advantages that we tend to squander through sprawl-promoting or openly racist policies, and more generally by loading the costs of same onto future generations. They are also the places where we can realize efficiencies in consumption costs, e.g. of housing, transportation, energy, health care. Housing, transportation, and utilities alone now account for better than 50 percent of median household expenditures, and close to 60 percent for households just below that median. For the latter, reducing these basic costs by a good-size amount, say a half, would amount to giving them a permanent 30 percent increase in disposable income. And properly organized metro can do just that. Denser development, mixed use (commercial and residential) neighborhoods, transit-based development, advanced education systems, easily realized energy savings, firms drawing on a common pool of skilled workers, easily realized energy savings, etc. etc. are all part of the mix here, realizing efficiencies in production and consumption.[24]

Rogers' point, which can be expanded on in a host of areas, is simple: the way we live is too expensive—both as a matter of what we shell out of our own pockets and, in the bigger sense, as a cost to the planet. We can change those costs dramatically—and, by doing so, make our lives economically easier without sacrificing quality of life, and, indeed, improving our quality of life.

In the end, there is a silver lining hidden behind the apprehensions and misgivings that most Americans feel today about the future. Even before the economic calamity of 2008, many workers had intuitively felt for some time that their world had changed forever, a world that rewarded you for working hard and playing by the rules. They had tended to express their anxiety through fears that their children, grandchildren and future generations would have a much tougher economic road to travel—though with things the way they are now, those fears are just as much for the present as for the future.

However, the clear failure of the so-called "free market" to bring fair distribution of the fruits of the labor of millions of people, coupled with the theft of hundreds of billions of dollars in wealth by a handful of people, have actually opened people up to a shift in values. This in turn has given us the ability to ignite a debate over a new economic vision, calling for a nationwide examination of our long-term economic policies here and abroad that rest on barreling forward blindly into the future. Rather than debate whether the economy is good or bad for us based solely on the number of jobs created—or lost—we have to challenge ourselves to rethink the organization of the economy so that, among other things, we don't accept the notion that the CEO is God and deserves Olympian rewards that bear no relationship to the difficulty or challenge of the job.

Ultimately, challenging the growth model means rejecting the prerogatives of capital, something we have accepted for generations. But, rejecting it can, and should, open up extremely difficult questions with no easy answers: for what purposes do we work? What does society want income from work to provide for? How does our standard of living clash with the ecological and economic realities of the globe?

Let the debate begin.

Acknowledgments

Robert Joseph Woods was a dogged and intrepid researcher who pulled together dossiers on the CEOs. Thanks to Robert Lasner and Elizabeth Clementson at Ig Publishing for realizing that this story was worth telling. Various people helped in small and big ways on this project. Alphabetically, they are: Dean Baker, Ron Blackwell, John Byrne, Bill Gibson, Roger Kerson, Ethel Klein, Ed Krugman, Terry Jones, George Lakoff, Carol Mithers, Dan Pedrotty, Joel Rogers, Heather Slavkin, Mark Weisbrot, and, out of order, all my friends at Blue Mountain Center.

Notes

Introduction

1. "Executive Pay: the Bottom Line for Those at the Top," *New York Times*, April 5, 2008, http://www.nytimes.com/interactive/2008/04/05/business/20080405_EXECCOMP_GRAPHIC. html?scp=6&sq=200%20chief%20executives%20&st=cse

2. Stephen Taub, "Best-Paid Hedge Fund Managers," *Alpha Magazine*, March 2008, http://www.iimagazine.com/article. aspx?articleID=1914753

3. "Paulson & Co. Scores Again This Year," by Gregory Zuckerman, *Wall Street Journal*, October 24, 2008.

4. Taub, "Best-Paid Hedge Fund Managers."

5. BBC News, "The man who broke the Bank of England," December 6, 1998, http://news.bbc.co.uk/1/hi/business/229012.stm

6. Noelle Barton and Peter Panepento, "Executive Pay Rises 4.6%," *Chronicle of Philanthropy* 19 no. 23 (September 20, 2007).

7. Ibid.

8. Edmund L. Andrews And Vikas Bajaj, "U.S. Plans $500,000 Cap on Executive Pay in Bailouts," *New York Times*, February 3, 2009, http://www.nytimes.com/2009/02/04/business/04pay.html?partner =rss&emc=rss&pagewanted=all

9. Louis Uchitelle, "The End of the Line as Detroit Workers Know It," *New York Times*, April 1, 2007, http://www.nytimes.com/2007/04/01/business/yourmoney/01jobs.html?ex=1333080000&en=b050d87e6

4dfce19&ei=5090&partner=rssuserland&emc=rss

10. Sarah Anderson, John Cavanagh, Chuck Collins and Eric Benjamin, "Executive Excess 2006: Defense and Oil Executives Cash in on Conflict," Institute for Policy Studies and United for a Fair Economy, August 2006, www.ips-dc.org/getfile.php?id=155

11. Jesse Drucker, "Richest Americans See Their Income Share Grow," *Wall Street Journal*, July 23, 2008.

12. Ibid.

1. Laying the Groundwork for the Looting of America

1. Longview Institute, "Market Fundamentalism," http://www.longviewinstitute.org/projects/marketfundamentalism/marketfundamentalism

2. Ibid.

3. Kristin Jensen and Mark Drajem, "Clinton Breaks With Husband's Legacy on Nafta Pact, China Trade," *Bloomberg*, March 30, 2007, http://www.bloomberg.com/apps/news?pid=20601070&sid=atUKcP4eSEvY&refer=politics

4. Sheryl Gay Stolberg and Robert Pear, "Bush Speaks in Defense of Markets," *New York Times*, November 14, 2008.

5. David Harvey, *A Brief History of NeoLiberalism*, (New York: Oxford University Press, 2005), 23.

6. Timothy Curry and Lynn Shibut, "The Cost of the Savings and Loan Crisis: Truth and Consequences," *FDIC Banking Review*, December 2000, http://www.fdic.gov/bank/analytical/banking/2000dec/brv13n2_2.pdf

7. Robert F. Kennedy, Jr., "Speech at the Sierra Summit" (speech, Sierra Club Convention, San Francisco, September 10, 2005) http://www.sierraclub.org/pressroom/speeches/2005-09-10rfkjr.asp

8. "Remarks of President Barack Obama – As Prepared for Delivery Address to Joint Session of Congress Tuesday, February 24th, 2009," http://www.whitehouse.gov/the_press_office/remarks-of-president-barack-obama-address-to-joint-session-of-congress/

9. This was actually an accusation hurled at me by Stephen Moore of the

Wall Street Journal editorial board during an April 30, 2009 debate on CNBC. "Unions Vs. Autocompanies," CNBC, April 30, 2009, http://www.cnbc.com/id/15840232?video=1109387073&play=1

10. Eric Dash and Louise Story, "Citigroup Tries to Stop the Drop in Its Share Price," *New York Times*, November 20, 2008, http://www.nytimes.com/2008/11/21/business/21finance.html?_r=1

11. Ibid.

12. Equilar, "CEO Compensation: Vikram S. Pandit," http://www.equilar.com/CEO_Compensation/Citigroup_Vikram_S._Pandit.php

13. Citigroup, "Citi Issues First Quarterly Progress Report on its Use of TARP Capital," press release, February 3, 2009, http://www.citigroup.com/citi/press/2009/090203a.htm

14. OECD Glossary of Statistical Terms, "Free Trade," August 26, 2004, http://stats.oecd.org/glossary/detail.asp?ID=6265

15. United States Department of Labor, Bureau of Labor Statistics, "Glossary," http://www.bls.gov/bls/glossary.htm#C

16. Robert Kuttner, "Rethinking Free Trade," *Boston Globe*, September 29, 2004, http://www.boston.com/news/globe/editorial_opinion/oped/articles/2004/09/29/rethinking_free_trade/

17. Gerald F. Seib, "Voters' tide turns toward support of Nafta, as debater Gore helps the pact, and vice versa," *Wall Street Journal*, November 17, 1993.

18. "NAFTA Debate: Gore vs. Perot," *Larry King Live*, CNN, November 9, 1993, Transcript # 961-1 http://ggallarotti.web.wesleyan.edu/govt155/goreperot.htm

19. Jagdish Bhagwati, "Obama's free-trade credentials top Clinton's," *Financial Times*, March 3, 2008.

20. Nina Easton, "Obama: NAFTA not so bad after all," *Fortune*, June 18, 2008, http://money.cnn.com/2008/06/18/magazines/fortune/easton_obama.fortune/index.htm?postversion=2008061810

21. John M. Broder, "Obama Opposes Trade Sanctions in Climate Bill," *New York Times*, June 28, 2009, http://www.nytimes.com/2009/06/29/us/politics/29climate.html?hp

22. Gary Clyde Hufbauer, Jeffrey J. Schott, Robin Dunnigan, Diana

Clark, *NAFTA: An Assessment*, (Washington D.C.: Institute for International Economics, 1993), 15.

23. Louis S. Richman, "How NAFTA Will Help America," *Fortune*, April 19, 1993, http://money.cnn.com/magazines/fortune/fortune_archive/1993/04/19/77742/index.htm

24. Jeff Faux, Carlos Salas, Robert E. Scott, "Revisiting NAFTA: Still not working for North America's workers," Economic Policy Institute, September 28, 2006, http://www.epi.org/publications/entry/bp173/

25. Congresswoman Marcy Kaptur, "America's Trade Deficit is on the Rise Again," May 12, 2009, http://www.kaptur.house.gov/index.php?option=com_content&task=view&id=439&Itemid=51

26. Public Citizen, "Trade Wars: Revenge of the Myth—Deals for Trade Votes Gone Bad," June 2005, 24, http://www.citizen.org/documents/tradewars.pdf

27. Ibid.

28. Ibid, 6.

29. Dean Baker and Mark Weisbrot, "Globalization, Productivity, and 'Protectionism," *International Business Times*, July 6, 2007, http://www.ibtimes.com/columns/title/MARK-WEISBROT/globalization-productivity-and-protectionism.htm

30. Mark Weisbrot, "Latin America: The End of an Era," *International Journal of Health Services* 36 no. 4 (Winter 2006), http://www.cepr.net/index.php?option=com_content&task=view&id=373

31. Robert Reich, "Building A New Middle Class," speech delivered on August 31, 1994 at the Center for National Policy, CSPAN (DVD),http://www.c-spanarchives.org/library/index.php?main_page=product_video_info&products_id=59935-1

32. Thomas L. Friedman, "The Green Road Less Traveled," *New York Times*, July 15, 2007.

33. Oded Shenkar, *The Chinese Century: The Rising Chinese Economy and It's Impact on the Global Economy, The Balance of Power, and Your Job*, (Upper Saddle River, New Jersey: Pearson Education, 2005) October 2004.

2. The Club

1. "Network Guerillas", by Guy de Jonquieres, *The Financial Times*, April 30, 1998, quoted in Lori Wallach and Patrick Woodall, *Whose Trade Organization?: A Comprehensive Guide To the WTO* (New York: New Press, 2004), 15.

2. Steven Greenhouse, "Trade Ministers Sidestep A Sticky Issue: Secrecy," *New York Times*, December 4, 1999, http://query.nytimes. com/gst/fullpage.html?res=9902E5D8153EF937A35751C1A96F 958260&n=Top/Reference/Times%20Topics/Organizations/W/ World%20Trade%20Organization

3. Robert Kuttner, "Friendly Takeover," *American Prospect*, March 18, 2007, http://www.prospect.org/cs/articles?articleId=12573

4. Rick Schmitt, "Prophet and Loss," *Stanford Magazine*, March/April 2009, http://www.stanfordalumni.org/news/magazine/2009/marapr/features/born.html

5. Peter S. Goodman, "Taking Hard New Look at a Greenspan Legacy," *New York Times*, October 8, 2008, http://www.nytimes.com/2008/10/09/business/economy/09greenspan.html?_r=1&em&oref=slogin

6. Ibid.

7. Ibid.

8. Dean Baker, "Short-Term Gain for Long-Term Pain: The Real Story of Rubinomics," Center for Economic and Policy Research (Paper presented at the Hofstra University 11th Presidential Conference: William Jefferson Clinton, the "New Democrat" from Hope, November 11, 2005), http://www.cepr.net/documents/publications/ financial_bubbles_2005_03_20.pdf

9. Ibid.

10. Robert Rubin, interview by Bob Schieffer, *Face The Nation*, CBS News, August 3, 2008, http://www.cbsnews.com/htdocs/pdf/ FTN_080308.pdf

11. Robert Rubin, interview by Bob Schieffer, *Face The Nation*, CBS News, October 26, 2008, http://www.cbsnews.com/htdocs/pdf/

FTN_102608.pdf

12. *Wall Street Journal*, "Editorial: No Line Responsibilities' What Robert Rubin did for his $115 million," December 3, 2008, http://online.wsj.com/article/SB122826632081174473.html

13. Ibid.

14. Ken Brown and David Enrich, "Rubin, Under Fire, Defends His Role at Citi," *Wall Street Journal*, November 29th 2008, http://online.wsj.com/article/SB122791795940965645.html

15. U.S. Department of Treasury, "Treasury Secretary Robert E. Rubin Remarks Before The World Economic Conference Davos, Switzerland," press release, January 30, 1999, http://www.ustreas.gov/press/releases/rr2920.htm

16. Brown and Enrich, "Rubin, Under Fire, Defends His Role at Citi."

17. Ibid.

18. Jo Becker and Gretchen Morgenson, "Geithner, Member and Overseer of Finance Club," *New York Times*, April 26, 2009, http://www.nytimes.com/2009/04/27/business/27geithner.html?hp

19. Marcella Bombardieri, "Summers' remarks on women draw fire," *Boston Globe*, January 17, 2005, http://www.boston.com/news/local/articles/2005/01/17/summers_remarks_on_women_draw_fire/

20. The Whirled Bank, "Laurence Summers: The Bank Memo," http://www.whirledbank.org/ourwords/summers.html

21. Schmitt, "Prophet and Loss."

22. Philip Rucker and Joe Stephens, "Top Economics Aide Discloses Income: Summers Earned Salary From Hedge Fund, Speaking Fees From Wall St. Firms," *Washington Post*, April 3, 2009, http://www.washingtonpost.com/wp-dyn/content/article/2009/04/03/AR2009040303732.html?hpid=topnews

3. Stock Option Scam

1. Donald P. Delves, *Stock Options And The New Rules Of Corporate Accountability*, (McGraw-Hill: New York, 2003), 27-29.

2. Felix Rohaytn, "Saving American Capitalism," *New York Times*, June 28, 2009, http://www.nytimes.com/2009/06/29/opinion/29iht-

edrohatyn.html?scp=2&sq=felix%20rohaytn&st=Search

3. All quotes from Graef Crystal are from author interview conducted in 2008.

4. John A. Byrne, "The CEO and the Board," *Business Week*, September 15, 1997, http://www.businessweek.com/1997/37/b3544001.htm

5. Ibid.

6. Mark Maremont and Charles Forelle, "Open Spigot: Bosses' Pay: How Stock Options Became Part of the Problem; Once Seen as a Reform, They Grew Into Font of Riches And System to Be Gamed; Reload, Reprice, Backdate," *Wall Street Journal*, December 27, 2006.

7. Joseph Blasi, Douglas Kruse and Aaron Bernstein, I*n The Company of Owners: The Truth about Stock Options (And Why Every Employee Should Have Them)*, (New York: Basic Books, 2003), 201.

8. Mark Maremont and Charles Forelle, "Open Spigot: Bosses' Pay: How Stock Options Became Part of the Problem; Once Seen as a Reform, They Grew Into Font of Riches And System to Be Gamed; Reload, Reprice, Backdate," *Wall Street Journal*, December 27, 2006.

9. Chad Bray, "Ex-Monster President Found Guilty in Backdating," *Wall Street Journal*, May 13, 2009.

10. Michael Corkery and Mark Maremont, "Corporate News: Former Chief of KB Home Indicted—Karatz Accused of Inflating Value of Stock-Options Grants and Hiding Scheme," *Wall Street Journal*, March 6, 2009.

11. Ibid.

12. *Forbes*, "Executive Pay: What the Boss Makes: Bruce Karatz," http://www.forbes.com/lists/2006/12/O29G.html

13. Building Online.com, "KB Home CEO Bruce Karatz Ousted in Stock Backdating Scandal," November 17, 2006, http://www.buildingonline.com/news/viewnews.pl?id=5605

14. Justin Scheck and Nick Wingfield, "Corporate News: Criminal Probe of Apple Options Is Ended; Justice Department Declines to File Charges Related to Backdating," *Wall Street Journal*, July 10, 2008.

15. Charles Forelle and James Bandler, "The Perfect Payday; Some CEOs reap millions by landing stock options when they are most valuable; Luck -- or something else?" *Wall Street Journal*, March 18, 2006.

16. U.S Securities and Exchange Commission, "Former UnitedHealth Group CEO/Chairman Settles Stock Options Backdating Case for $468 Million," press release, December 6, 2007, http://www.sec.gov/news/press/2007/2007-255.htm

17. Dan Slater, "UnitedHealth Settles 'Historical Stock Options Practices' Case for $895 Mil," *Wall Street Journal*, July 2, 2008, http://blogs.wsj.com/law/2008/07/02/unitedhealth-settles-historical-stock-options-practices-case-for-890-mil/

18. Ibid.

19. Mark Maremont and Charles Forelle, "Open Spigot."

20. M. P. Narayanan, Cindy A. Schipani and H. Nejat Seyhun, "The Economic Impact of Backdating of Executive Stock Options," *Michigan Law Review* 105, no. 8 (June 2007).

21. M. P. Narayanan and H. Nejat Seyhun, "Do Managers Influence their Pay? Evidence from stock price reversals around executive option grants," University of Michigan, January 2005, http://sitemaker.umich.edu/options-backdating/files/050117execoptions.pdf

22. M. P. Narayanan and H. Nejat Seyhun, "The Dating Game: Do Managers Designate Option Grant Dates to Increase Their Compensation?" *The Review of Financial Studies* 21 no. 5 (September 2008), 1907-1945.

23. Mark Maremont and Charles Forelle, "Bosses' Pay: How Stock Options Became Part of the Problem," *Wall Street Journal*, December 27, 2006.

4. Vodka and Penises

1. CNNMoney.com, "Jurors see tape of Kozlowski's party," October 29, 2003, http://money.cnn.com/2003/10/28/news/companies/tyco_party/

2. Annelena Lobb, "Shop like Dennis K," CNNMoney.com, September

24, 2002, http://money.cnn.com/2002/09/23/pf/saving/q_tyco/

3. Ben White, "Tyco Report Paints Picture Of Greed: CEO Kozlowski Allegedly Deceived Firm's Board," *Washington Post*, September 18, 2002, http://www.washingtonpost.com/ac2/wp-dyn/A31362-2002Sep17?language=printer

4. Alex Berenson and Carol Vogel, "Ex-Tyco Chief Is Indicted In Tax Case," *New York Times*, June 5, 2002; Tracy Connor,"The Lucky Women Of Koz Ex-Tyco boss lavishes gifts on his ladies," *New York Daily News*, November 2003, http://www.nydailynews.com/archives/news/2003/11/02/2003-11-02__the_lucky_women_of_koz__ex-.htm

5. Andrew Ross Sorkin, "Tyco Details Lavish Lives Of Executives," *New York Times*, September 18, 2002.

6. Andrew Ross Sorkin and Jennifer Bayo,"Ex-Tyco Officers Get 8 to 25 Years," *New York Times*, September 20, 2005.

7. Brooke Masters and Francesco Guerrera, "Tyco to pay $3bn to settle with shareholders," *Financial Times*, May 15, 2007,http://www.ft.com/cms/s/0/f5f78f66-02ff-11dc-a023-000b5df10621.html?nclick_check=1

8. Anthony Bianco, William Symonds, and Nanette Byrnes, "The Rise and Fall of Dennis Kozlowski," *Business Week*, December 23, 2002, http://www.businessweek.com/print/magazine/content/02_51/b3813001.htm?chan=mz

9. *United States vs. Bernard J. Ebbers and Scott D. Sullivan*, U.S.D.C. S.D. NY, S3 02 Cr. 1144 (BSJ), http://www.cbsnews.com/htdocs/pdf/ebbie.pdf

10. Ken Belson, Jonathan Glater, Gretchen Morgenson and Colin Moynihan,"Ex-Chief of WorldCom Is Found Guilty in $11 Billion Fraud," *New York Times*, March 16, 2005.

11. Luisa Beltran,"WorldCom files largest bankruptcy ever . Nation's No. 2 long-distance company in Chapter 11 -- largest with $107 billion in assets," CNN/Money, July 22, 2002, http://money.cnn.com/2002/07/19/news/worldcom_bankruptcy/

12. *United States vs. Bernard J. Ebbers and Scott D. Sullivan.*

13. Steve Rosenbush, "The Message In Ebber's Sentence," *Business Week*, July 14, 2005, http://www.businessweek.com/technology/content/jul2005/tc20050714_0826_tc062.htm

14. U.S. Securities and Exchange Commission, "SEC Charges Adelphia and Rigas Family With Massive Financial Fraud," press release, July 24, 2002, http://www.sec.gov/news/press/2002-110.htm

15. Ibid.

16. Andrew Ross Sorkin, "Adelphia Is Next in Parade of Fraud Trials," *New York Times*, February 23, 2004; Barry Meier, "Portrait of a Family, as Painted at a Fraud Trial," New York Times, May 30, 2004.

17. Barry Meier, "Witness Tells of Dual Accounting at Adelphia," *New York Times*, May 5, 2004, http://query.nytimes.com/gst/fullpage.html?res=9B01E4DF1E3DF936A35756C0A9629C8B63

18. CNN/Money, "Adelphia founder sentenced to 15 years," June 20, 2005, http://money.cnn.com/2005/06/20/news/newsmakers/rigas_sentencing/

19. *New York Times*, "Son of Adelphia Founder Guilty of Falsifying Records," November 24, 2005.

20. Roger Lowenstein, "The Company They Kept," *New York Times Sunday Magazine*, February 1, 2004, http://query.nytimes.com/gst/fullpage.html?res=9D07E1D71738F932A35751C0A9629C8B63

21. Bloomberg News, "Deloitte and Banks to Pay $455 Million to Adelphia Investors", *New York Times*, December 9, 2006, http://www.nytimes.com/2006/12/09/business/09adelphia.html

22. Dan Ackman, "House Committees To Investigate Global Crossing," *Forbes*, March 13, 2002, http://www.forbes.com/2002/03/13/0313topnews.html

23. Jeff Gerth, "Clinton's Top Fund-Raiser Made Lots for Himself, Too," *New York Times*, December 12, 1999.

24. Simon Romero, "Global Crossing Head Offers Workers $25 Million," *New York Times*, October 2, 2002.

25. Simon Romero, "Global Crossing Memo Indicates Early Warning Of Downfall," *New York Times*, October 1, 2002.

26. Chris Gaither, Jonathan Peterson, and David Colker, "Founder Es-

capes Charges in Global Crossing Failure, *Los Angeles Times*, December 14, 2004, http://articles.latimes.com/2004/dec/14/business/fi-winnick14

27. *Newshour with Jim Lehrer*, "The Long Fall," March 21, 2002, PBS, http://www.pbs.org/newshour/bb/business/jan-june02/crossing_3-21.html

28. The Winnick Foundation, http://www.winnickfoundation.com/

29. Edward Iwata, "Payouts Anger Former Enron Workers," *USA Today*, June 18, 2002.

30. Bethany McLean, "Is Enron Overpriced?", *Fortune*, March 5, 2001 http://money.cnn.com/2006/01/13/news/companies/enronoriginal_fortune/index.htm?postversion=2006011818

31. "Enron and Campaign Finance Reform," Public Citizen, January 24, 2002, http://www.citizen.org/congress/campaign/legislation/bcralaw/articles.cfm?ID=6693

32. M. Asif Ismail, "A Most Favored Corporation: Enron Prevailed in Federal, State Lobbying Efforts 49 Times," The Center for Public Integrity, January 06, 2003 http://www.publicintegrity.org/articles/entry/379/

33. Christian Zappone, "Ex-Enron workers rejoice after verdicts", CNNMoney.com, May 25, 2006, http://money.cnn.com/2006/05/25/news/newsmakers/enron_reaction/

34. Carrie Johnson, "Former Enron CEO Lay Surrenders in Houston: Lay Enters Not Guilty Plea to All Charges," *Washington Post*, July 8, 2004, http://www.washingtonpost.com/wp-dyn/articles/A36129-2004Jul8.html

35. Gretchen Morgenson, "Remember When Ken Lay Was a Genius?," *New York Times*, January 16, 2005.

36. Andrew Ross Sorkin, "Ex-Chief and Aide Guilty Of Looting Millions At Tyco," *New York Times*, June 18, 2005.

5. The Retirement Jackpot

1. Tomoeh Murakami Tse, "Long-Serving AT&T Chief To Leave With Huge Payout," *Washington Post*, April 28, 2007; U.S. Securi-

ties and Exchange Commission, "AT&T Proxy Statement Pursuant to Section 14(a), March 22," 2007, http://phx.corporate-ir.net/phoenix.zhtml?c=113088&p=irol-SECText&TEXT=aHR0cDov L2NjYm4uMTBrd2l6YXJkLmNvbS94bWwvZmlsaW5nLnhtbD 9yZXBvPXRRlbmsmaXBhZ2U9U9NDc2MDg4OSZkb2M9MSZud W09NTA%3d

2. Matthew Kirdahy, "CEO Pensions Continue To Soar," May 7 2007, http://www.forbes.com/2007/05/07/ceo-pensions-whitacre-lead-manage-cx_mk_0503pensions.html

3. Barry Burr, "Pension goldmine awaits AT&T, Occidental CEOs," *Pension&Investments*, April 2, 2007, http://www.pionline.com/apps/pbcs.dll/article?AID=/20070402/PRINTSUB/70330045&nocache=1

4. U.S. Securities and Exchange Commission, "SEC Votes to Adopt Changes to Disclosure Requirements Concerning Executive Compensation and Related Matters," press release, July 26, 2006, http://www.sec.gov/news/press/2006/2006-123.htm

5. Mary Williams Walsh, "New Rules Urged to Avert Looming Pension Crisis," *New York Times*, July 28, 2003.

6. Marilyn Adams and Sue Kirchhoff, "Pension crisis comes to head with vote today," *USA Today*, April 2, 2004.

7. Heron Marquez Estrada, "Star Tribune sues union to try to void pension deal," *Star Tribune*, May 18, 2009.

8. Nicole Harris, Theo Francis and Ellen Schultz, "Delta CEO Mullin Will Forgo Millions in His Compensation," *Wall Street Journal*, April 4, 2003.

9. Janice Revell, "CEO Pensions: The Latest Way To Hide Millions Think CEO pay is out of control? Wait till you see what these guys get when they retire," *Fortune*, April 28, 2003, http://money.cnn.com/magazines/fortune/fortune_archive/2003/04/28/341732/index.htm

10. Ellen E. Schultz and Theo Francis, "Hidden Burden: As Workers' Pensions Wither, Those for Executives Flourish; Companies Run Up Big IOUs, Mostly Obscured, to Grant Bosses a Lucrative Benefit; The Billion-Dollar Liability," *Wall Street Journal*, June 23, 2006.

11. David Welch, Dan Beucke, Kathleen Kerwin, Michael Arndt, Brian Hindo, Emily Thornton, David Kiley and Ian Rowley, "Why GM's Plan Won't Work," *Business Week*, May 9, 2005, http.//www.businessweek.com/magazine/content/05_19/b3932001_mz001.htm

12. Ellen E. Schultz and Theo Francis, "Hidden Burden: As Workers' Pensions Wither, Those for Executives Flourish; Companies Run Up Big IOUs, Mostly Obscured, to Grant Bosses a Lucrative Benefit; The Billion-Dollar Liability," *Wall Street Journal*, June 23, 2006.

13. Ibid.

14. Ibid.

15. Ellen E. Schultz, "Banks Owe Billions to Executives," *Wall Street Journal*, October 31, 2008.

16. Mark Maremont, "How Some Firms Boost the Boss's Pension," *Wall Street Journal*, January 23, 2009.

17. Ibid.

18. Ellen E. Schultz, "Banks Use Life Insurance to Fund Bonuses---Controversial Policies on Employees Pay for Executive Benefits, Help Companies With Taxes," *Wall Street Journal*, May 20, 2009.

19. Ibid.

20. Ellen E. Schultz and Theo Francis, "Companies Tap Pension Plans To Fund Executive Benefits; Little-Known Move Uses Tax Break Meant for Rank and File," *Wall Street Journal*, August 4, 2008.

21. Ibid.

22. Ibid.

23. Robin Talbert, "Commentary and Opinion: On the Road to An Aging America," Philanthropy News Digest, March 16, 2007, http://foundationcenter.org/pnd/commentary/co_item.jhtml?id=173200044

24. Employee Benefit Research Institute, "401(k) Plan Asset Allocation, Account Balances, and Loan Activity in 2007," EBRI Issue Brief #324, December 2008, http://www.ebri.org/publications/ib/index.cfm?fa=ibDisp&content_id=4132

25. *Wall Street Journal*, "Americans Delay Retirement as Housing Stocks Swoon," April 1, 2008.

26. Mauricio Soto, "How Is the Financial Crisis Affecting Retirement

Savings?", The Urban Institute, May 14, 2009, http://www.urban.
org/retirement_policy/url.cfm?ID=411880

27. Nancy Trejos, "Retirement Wreck: Are 401(k)s Still Viable for Saving?" *Washington Post*, October 12, 2008, http://www.washingtonpost.
com/wp-dyn/content/article/2008/10/11/AR2008101100177.
html?referrer=emailarticle

28. Ibid.

29. U.S. House Committe on Education and Labor, "The Impact of
the Financial Crisis on Workers' Retirement Security," Statement
by Roberta Tim Quan, 110th Cong., 2nd sess., October 22, 2008,
http://edlabor.house.gov/testimony/2008-10-22-RobertaQuan.pdf

30. U.S. House Committe on Education and Labor, "The Impact of
the Financial Crisis on Workers' Retirement Security," Statement
by Steve Carroll, 110th Cong., 2nd sess., October 22, 2008, http://
edlabor.house.gov/testimony/2008-10-22-SteveCarroll.pdf

6. How to Screw Up Your Company—And Still Get Rich

1. Gretchen Morgenson, "Fair Game; A Lump Of Coal Might Suffice,"
New York Times, December 24, 2006

2. *Forbes*, "CEO Compensation: Henry A McKinnell," http://www.
forbes.com/lists/2006/12/EYQ9.html

3. Ylan Q. Mui, "Seeing Red Over a Golden Parachute: Home Depot's
CEO Resigns, And His Hefty Payout Raises Ire," *Washington Post*,
Thursday, January 4, 2007.

4. Ibid.

5. Brian Grow, "Out at Home Depot," *Business Week*, January 9, 2007,
http://www.msnbc.msn.com/id/16469224/

6. Ibid.

7. Del Jones and Matt Krantz, "Home Depot boots CEO Nardelli",
USA Today, January 4, 2007, http://www.usatoday.com/money/industries/retail/2007-01-03-hd-nardelli_x.htm

8. Andy Serwer and Ann Harrington, "Frank Newman Feels the Heat,"
Fortune, October 26, 1998, http://money.cnn.com/magazines/fortune/fortune_archive/1998/10/26/249977/index.htm

9. Ibid.

10. *New York Daily News*, "A Huge Parachute Bankers Trust CEO May Land With 100m," June 30 1999, http://www.nydailynews.com/archives/money/1999/06/30/1999-06-30_a_huge_parachute_bankers_tru.html

11. Gretchen Morgenson, "A Public Pension Fund Sues Directors of Caremark Rx," *New York Times*, January 11, 2007.

12. CtW Investment Group, "Failed Oversight," http://www.ctwinvestmentgroup.com/index.php?id=27

13. Richard Verrier, "Ovitz Case Haunts Disney Board," *Los Angeles Times*, September 20, 2004.

14. AFL-CIO, "Citigroup Case Study," http://www.aflcio.org/corporatewatch/paywatch/retirementsecurity/case_citigroup.cfm

15. Jeffrey McCracken, "UAW Files Protest To Delphi Bonuses For Top Executives," *Wall Street Journal*, November 25, 2005.

16. Ibid.

17. Claudia H. Deutsch And Joseph B. Treaster, "Corporate Conduct: The Reaction; Other Executives Voice Satisfaction at Arrests," *New York Times*, July 25, 2002, http://query.nytimes.com/gst/fullpage.html?res=9B01E0DB1038F936A15754C0A9649C8B63

18. Gretchen Morgenson, "Royal Pay at Delphi, Reined in by a Judge," *New York Times*, January 27, 2008,
http://www.nytimes.com/2008/01/27/business/27gret.html?ex=1359090000&en=6c48ce5b0596b7de&ei=5090&partner=rssuserland&emc=rss&pagewanted=all

19. Andrew Ross Sorkin, "Lehman Files for Bankruptcy; Merrill Is Sold," *New York Times*, September 14, 2008. http://www.nytimes.com/2008/09/15/business/15lehman.html?hp

20. *Fortune*, "101 Dumbest Moments in Business: 5. Stanley O'Neal," http://money.cnn.com/galleries/2007/fortune/0712/gallery.101_dumbest.fortune/5.html

21. Equilar, "CEO Compensation for John A. Thain," http://www.equilar.com/CEO_Compensation/MERRILL_LYNCH_AND_CO_INC_John_A._Thain.php

22. Susanne Craig, "Thain Spars With Board Over Bonus At Merrill," *Wall Street Journal*, December 8, 2008.

23. Helen Kennedy, "Former Merrill Lynch CEO John Thain resigns from Bank of America amid bonus scandal," *New York Daily News*, January 22, 2009, http://www.nydailynews.com/money/2009/01/22/2009-01-22_former_merrill_lynch_ceo_john_thain_resi.html

24. Greg B. Smith, "Cuomo reveals 4 top Merrill Lynch execs grabbed big bucks just before government-financed takeover," *New York Daily News*, February 11 2009.

25. Daniel Gross, "The Golden Ass: How Blackstone CEO Steve Schwarzman's antics may cost him and his colleagues billions of dollars," *Slate*, June 19, 2007, http://www.slate.com/id/2168650; "Blackstone Posts $93 Million Loss," *New York Times*, May 6, 2009, http://dealbook.blogs.nytimes.com/2009/05/06/blackstone-posts-93-million-loss/

26. U.S. Securities and Exchange Commission, "Blackstone Group, LP Annual Report for the fiscal year ended Dec 31, 2007," March 6, 2008, http://www.sec.gov/Archives/edgar/data/1393818/000119312508053079/d10k.htm#toc

27. U.S. Securities and Exchange Commission, "Stephen A Schwarzman Initial Statement of Beneficial Ownership of Securities," (June 21, 2007), http://www.sec.gov/Archives/edgar/data/1070844/000089375007000242/xslF345X02/form3_ex.xml

28. U.S. Securities and Exchange Commission, "Blackstone Group, LP Annual Report for the fiscal year ended Dec 31, 2007."

29. Blackstone's common units closed at $5.94 on December 26, 2008. As of February 19, 2009, the 52-week low was $4.05 per common unit. See Google Finance at http://www.google.com/finance?q=bx

30. U.S. Securities and Exchange Commission, "Blackstone Group, LP Annual Report for the fiscal year ended Dec 31, 2007."

31. U.S. Securities and Exchange Commission, "Blackstone Group, LP Annual Report for the fiscal year ended Dec 31, 2007."

32. Daniel Gross, "The Golden Ass: How Blackstone CEO Steve

Schwarzman's antics may cost him and his colleagues billions of dollars," *Slate*, June 19, 2007, http://www.slate.com/id/2168650

33. James B. Stewart, "The Birthday Party: How Stephen Schwarzman became private equity's designated villain," *New Yorker*, February 11, 2008.

34. U.S. Securities and Exchange Commission, "Blackstone Group LP Quarterly Report for the period ended June 30, 2008,"http://www.sec. gov/Archives/edgar/data/1393818/000119312508171618/d10q. htm; U.S. Securities and Exchange Commission, "Blackstone Group LP Quarterly Report for the period ended September 30, http://www. sec.gov/Archives/edgar/data/1393818/000119312508229980/ d10q.htm

35. Michael Flaherty and Narayanan Somasundaram, "Investing in India? See Blackstone losses," *Reuters*, January 21, 2009, http://uk.reuters. com/article/innovationNews/idUKTRE50J1N320090121?sp=true.

36. *Reuters*, "Blackstone to liquidate two hedge funds," December 23, 2008, http://uk.reuters.com/article/marketsNewsUS/ idUKN2354961920081223.

37. Kimi Yoshino, "Hilton Hotels receives a new chief executive," *Los Angeles Times*, October 30, 2007, http://articles.latimes.com/2007/ oct/30/business/fi-hilton30.

38. Goldman Sachs, "The Blackstone Group LP: Long-term value beset by near-term challenges – initiate at Neutral," November 25, 2008.

39. *David Galchutt et. al. v. The Blackstone Group LP, Stephen A. Schwarzman and Michael A. Puglisi*, Class Action Complaint for Violation of Federal Securities Laws, U.S.D.C. S.D. NY Case 1:08-cv-04110-HB.

40. *Forbes*, "The World's Billionaires: #145 Stephen Schwarzman," http://www.forbes.com/lists/2008/10/billionaires08_Stephen-Schwarzman_KH57.html

41. Peter Lattman, "Depression' Pinch Buffets Blackstone," *Wall Street Journal*, Febraury 28, 2009.

42. Elizabeth Douglass, Karen Kaplan and James S. Granelli, "Global Crossing Hurt by Board's Cronyism; Telecom: Instability and lack

of independence among members may have hampered their ability to keep the company out of trouble," *Los Angeles Times*, February 24, 2002.

43. Ibid.

44. Ibid.

45. Data available in FedEx's filings at the U.S. Securities and Exchange Commission, http://www.sec.gov/edgar/searchedgar/company-search.html

46. Report by International Brotherhood of Teamsters, "It's Time For Board Independence at FedEx," September 2009.

47. Ibid.

48. James Surowiecki, "Board Stiff," *New Yorker*, June 1, 2009, 34.

49. *Derrick Satchell et al. v Fedex Express*, Case No. C 03-2659 & C 03-2878, http://www.fedexwatch.com/resources/content/satchell_et_al_vs_fedex_express/

50. Payscale.com, "Hourly Rate Survey Report for Employer: FedEx / Federal Express Corporation," http://www.payscale.com/research/US/Employer=FedEx_%2f_Federal_Express_Corporation/Hourly_Rate

51. FedEx Watch, "FedEx Announces Retirement Contribution Freeze," http://fedexwatch.com/content/pages/fedex_announces_retirement_contribution_freeze/

52. Employee Benefit Research Institute, "Historical Statistics – Benefit Statistics 1974-1978-2003," www.ebri.org/pdf/programs/policyforums/may2004/hbstats.pdf

53. Powerpoint Presentation by Damon Silvers, Associate General Counsel AFL-CIO.

54. Ibid.

55. Ibid.

56. AFL-CIO, "FedEx Corp. Case Study," http://www.aflcio.org/corporatewatch/paywatch/retirementsecurity/case_fedex.cfm#_ftn3

7. The Wage Cupboard Is Bare

1. Thomas Kochan, "Wages and the Social Contract," *American Prospect*,

April 22, 2007, http://www.prospect.org/cs/articles?article=wages_ and_the_social_contract

2. Ibid.

3. Lawrence Mishel and Jared Bernstein, "Productivity growth and profits far outpace compensation in current expansion," Economic Policy Institute, April 21, 2005, http://www.epinet.org/content. cfm/webfeatures_snapshots_20050421

4. Memo from Joel Rogers, Director of the Center on Wisconsin Strategy to author.

5. Ibid.

6. House Committee on Education and Labor, "Building an Economic Recovery Package: Creating and Preserving Jobs in America,"Testimony of Ron Blackwell, Chief Economist, American Federation of Labor and Congress of Industrial Organizations, 110th Cong., 2nd sess., October 24, 2008, http://edlabor.house.gov/testimony/2008-10-24-RonBlackwell.pdf

7. Ibid, 7.

8. Ibid, 8.

9. Gerald Prante, "Summary of Latest Federal Individual Income Tax Data," Tax Foundation, July 18, 2008, http://www.taxfoundation. org/news/show/250.html

10. Lawrence Mishel, Jared Bernstein, and Heidi Shierholz, *The State of Working America 2008/2009* (Washington D.C.: Economic Policy Institute, 2008), 6, http://www.stateofworkingamerica.org/ swa08_00_execsum.pdf

11. U.S. Department of Health and Human Services, "The 2009 HHS Poverty Guidelines," February 27, 2009, http://aspe.hhs.gov/ poverty/09poverty.shtml

12. U.S. Department of Labor, "History of Federal Minimum Wage Rates Under the Fair Labor Standards Act, 1938 – 2007." http:// www.dol.gov/ESA/minwage/chart.htm; U.S. Census Bureau, "Poverty Thresholds 2006," http://www.census.gov/hhes/www/poverty/ threshld/thresh06.html

13. For much more details about the Wal-Mart saga, visit Wal-Mart

Watch, www.walmartwatch.com, or Wake-Up Walmart, www. wakeupwalmart.com. There are also a good set of books on Wal-Mart, including *The Wal-Mart Effect* by Charles Fishman, *The Bully of Bentonville* by Anthony Bianco, *Selling Women Short: The Landmark Battle for Worker's Rights at Wal-Mart* by Liza Featherstone and *Nickel and Dimed: On (Not) Getting By in America* by Barbara Ehrenreich.

14. Forbes, "The 400 Richest Americans," http://www.forbes.com/lists/2008/54/400list08_The-400-Richest-Americans_NameProper_16.html

15. Human Rights Watch, "US: Wal-Mart Denies Workers Basic Rights," April 30, 2007, http://www.hrw.org/en/news/2007/04/30/us-wal-mart-denies-workers-basic-rights

16. Human Rights Watch, "Discounting Rights: Wal-Mart's Violation of US Workers' Right to Freedom of Association," April 30, 2007, http://hrw.org/en/reports/2007/04/30/discounting-rights

17. Frank Swoboda, "Wal-Mart Ends Meat-Cutting Jobs; Shutdown at 180 Stores Comes After a Union Victory," *Washington Post*, March 4, 2000.

18. Jared Bernstein and Josh Bivens, "The Wal-Mart debate: A false choice between prices and wages," Economic Policy Institute, June 15, 2006, http://www.epi.org/content.cfm/ib223

19. Stephan J. Goetz and Hema Swaminathan, "Wal-Mart and Country-Wide Poverty," October 18, 2004, Department of Agricultural Economics and Rural Sociology Pennsylvania State University, http://cecd.aers.psu.edu/pubs/PovertyResearchWM.pdf

20. Reuters, "Class-Action Bias Suit Against Wal-Mart Reaffirmed," *New York Times*, December 12, 2007, http://www.nytimes.com/2007/12/12/business/12bias.html?_r=1&ref=business&oref=slogin

21. Joe Schneider and Margaret Cronin Fisk, "Wal-Mart to Pay $54 Million to Settle Minnesota Suit," *Bloomberg News*, December 9, 2008, http://www.bloomberg.com/apps/news?pid=newsarchive&sid=aCAT7DH32w4o

22. For a compilation of news stories on the settlement, see Walmart Watch, "Wal-Mart Agrees To Pay $33 Million In Back Wages," http://walmartwatch.com/blog/archives/wal_mart_agrees_to_pay_33_million_in_back_wages/

23. Wakeup Walmart, "Finally, Wal-Mart Does the Right Thing," http://www.wakeupwalmart.com/feature/wmt_drops_case/

24. Letter from Pat Curran to James A. Shank, April 1, 2008, http://blog.wakeupwalmart.com/ufcw/wmt_shank_letter.pdf

25. Carol Vogel, "New York Public Library's Durand Painting Sold to Wal-Mart Heiress," *New York Times*, May 13, 2005, http://www.nytimes.com/2005/05/13/nyregion/13painting.html?

26. Wal-Mart Watch, "Issues: Health Care," http://walmartwatch.com/issues/health_care/

27. Cheryl Powell, "Public pays health care for private workers. Thousands at work in Ohio, many for big companies, must use Medicaid. Why? No employer medical plan," *Akron Beacon Journal*, September 1, 2008.

28. Susan Chambers, "Reviewing and Revising Wal-Mart's Benefits Strategy: Memorandum to the Board of Directors," Walmart Watch, http://walmartwatch.com/img/sitestream/docs/Susan_Chambers_Memo_to_Wal-Mart_Board.pdf

29. Wakeup Walmart, "Stop the Wal-Mart Health Care Crisis," http://wakeupwalmart.com/feature/healthcrisis/

30. Ibid.

31. Jesse Drucker, "Friendly Landlord: Wal-Mart Cuts Taxes By Paying Rent To Itself; Other Retailers, Banks Use Loophole in Rules To Lower States' Levies," *Wall Street Journal*, February 1, 2007.

32. Ibid.

33. Jesse Drucker, "Politics and Economics: Judge Rules Against Wal-Mart Over Its Tax-Shelter Dispute," *Wall Street Journal*, January 5, 2008.

34. Jesse Drucker, "Inside Wal-Mart's Bid To Slash State Taxes; Ernst & Young Devises Complex Strategies; California Pushes Back," *Wall Street Journal*, October 23, 2007.

35. Ibid.
36. Ibid.
37. Steven Greenhouse, "Labor Dept. To Investigate Its Treatment Of Wal-Mart," *New York Times*, February 21, 2005.
38. Ibid.
39. *New York Times*, "Inspection Pact Ends For Wal-Mart Stores," January 19, 2006.
40. Ibid.
41. Wal-Mart, "Wal-Mart Issues 2008 Annual Report & Proxy to Shareholders," April 22, 2008, press release, http://walmartstores.com/FactsNews/NewsRoom/8224.aspx
42. Michael Barbaro, "A New Weapon for Wal-Mart: A War Room," *New York Times*, November 1, 2005, http://www.nytimes.com/2005/11/01/business/01walmart.ready.html?hp&ex=1130907600&en=af9d3a977705cc52&ei=5094&partner=homepage
43. Open Secrets, "Wal-Mart Stores Contributions to Federal Candidates,"http://www.opensecrets.org/pacs/pacgot.php?cmte=C00093054&cycle=2008
44. Ann Zimmerman and Kris Maher, "Wal-Mart Warns of Democratic Win, *Wall Street Journal*, August 1, 2008, http://online.wsj.com/article/SB121755649066303381.html?mod=hps_us_whats_news
45. Kathleen Madigan, "More Firms Cut Pay to Save Jobs," *Wall Street Journal*, June 9, 2009, http://online.wsj.com/article/SB124450717216996329.html
6. Jonathan Tasini, "Pay Cuts—The New Rage," Daily Kos, June 9, 2009, http://www.dailykos.com/story/2009/6/9/740412/-Pay-CutsThe-New-Rage

8. The Great Collapse

1. *CBS News*, "Stocks Take Record Tumble, Down 777 Points," September 29, 2008, http://www.cbsnews.com/stories/2008/09/29/national/main4485321.shtml
2. Alexandra Twin, "Stocks Crashed," CNNMoney.com, September 29, 2008, http://money.cnn.com/2008/09/29/markets/markets_newy-

ork/index.htm

3. Dan Levy, "U.S. Property Owners Lost $3.3 Trillion in Home Value," *Bloomberg*, February 3, 2009, http://www.bloombcrg.com/apps/new s?pid=20601068&sid=aE29HSrxA4rI

4. Kirk Shinkle, "Damage Report 2008: Household Wealth Down $10 Trillion," *U.S. News and World Report*, December 12, 2008, http:// www.usnews.com/blogs/the-ticker/2008/12/12/damage-report-2008-household-wealth-down-10-trillion.html

5. Michael Hudson, "The New Road to Serfdom," *Harper's*, May 2006.

6. Stephen Mihm, "Dr. Doom," *New York Times Magazine*, August 15, 2008,http://www.nytimes.com/2008/08/17/magazine/17pessimist-t.html

7. Gretchen Morgenson, "Inside the Countrywide Lending Spree," *New York Times*, August 26, 2007, http://www.nytimes.com/2007/08/26/ business/yourmoney/26country.html

8. Reuters,"A Losing Year at Countrywide, but Not for Chief," *New York Times*, April 25, 2008, http://www.nytimes.com/2008/04/25/ business/25pay.html?adxnnl=1&adxnnlx=1225051363-rR81Ed-z1UwcisS8wzFRX2w

9. Paul Muolo and Mathew Padila, *Chain of Blame: How Wall Street Caused the Mortgage and Credit Crisis*, (Hoboken, NJ: John Wiley &. Sons, 2008), 255.

10. Gretchen Morgenson,"Inside the Countrywide Lending Spree,"*New York Times*, August 26, 2007, http://www.nytimes.com/2007/08/26/ business/yourmoney/26country.html

11. Gretchen Morgenson and Geraldine Fabrikant, "Countrywide's Chief Salesman And Defender," *New York Times*, November 11, 2007, http://query.nytimes.com/gst/fullpage.html?res=9A03E6D E1F3AF932A25752C1A9619C8B63&sec=&spon=&pagewante d=5

12. Ibid.

13. Ibid.

14. Ibid.

15. William Heisel, "Fannie Mac and Freddic Mac CEOs to get Gold

en Parachutes," *Los Angeles Times*, September 9, 2008, http://www.latimes.com/business/la-fi-fannie9-2008sep09,0,4063126.story

16. Mark Maremont, John Hechinger, Maurice Tamman, "Before the Bust, These CEOs Took Money Off the Table," *Wall Street Journal*, November 20, 2008.

17. Ibid.

18. Louise Story, "On Wall Street, Bonuses, Not Profits, Were Real," *New York Times*, December 18, 2008, http://www.nytimes.com/2008/12/18/business/18pay.html?em

19. Peter S. Goodman and Gretchen Morgenson, "Saying Yes, WaMu Built Empire on Shaky Loans," *New York Times*, December 27, 2008.

20. Ibid.

21. Bill Virgin, "WaMu laying off 3,000, cutting dividend," *Seattle Post-Intelligencer*, April 8, 2008, http://www.seattlepi.com/business/358278_wamu09.html

22. AFL-CIO, "Washington Mutual Case Study," http://www.aflcio.org/corporatewatch/paywatch/retirementsecurity/case_washmutual.cfm

23. Michael Brush, "WaMu: Skip customers; save the execs," MSN.com, March 19, 2008, http://articles.moneycentral.msn.com/Investing/CompanyFocus/WaMuSkipCustomersSaveTheExecs.aspx

24. Ibid.

25. Kirsten Grind, "Insiders detail reasons for WaMu's failure," *Jacksonville Business Journal*, January 29, 2009, http://www.bizjournals.com/jacksonville/stories/2009/01/26/daily30.html

26. Steven Church, "IRS says WaMu owes $12.5 billion" *Bloomberg News*, January 23, 2009.

27. Alistair Barr, "Bank Death Threat Suspect Arrested," *Market Watch*, February 3, 2009, http://www.marketwatch.com/story/suspect-arrested-over-powder-filled-mail

28. Pierre Thomas and Lauren Pearle, "WaMu Insiders Claim Execs Ignored Warnings, Encouraged Reckless Lending," *ABC News*, October 13, 2008, http://abcnews.go.com/TheLaw/

story?id=6021608&page=1

29. Rick Rothacker, "Golden West deal doomed Wachovia in crisis," *Charlotte Observer*, December 22, 2008, http://www.charlotteobserver.com/597/story/427887.html

30. Equilar, "CEO Compensation: G. Kennedy Thompson," http://www.equilar.com/CEO_Compensation/WACHOVIA_CORP_G._Kennedy_Thompson.php

31. E. Scott Reckard, "Wells Fargo suffering from weight of Wachovia's losses" *Los Angeles Times*, January 28, 2009, http://www.latimes.com/business/la-fi-wells28-2009jan28,0,3285858.story?track=rss

32. Irene Kan, "Countrywide's Campaign Contributions Weren't Loans, But They Were Investments," Open Secrets, June 18, 2008, http://www.opensecrets.org/news/2008/06/countrywides-campaign-contribu.html

33. Ibid.

34. Raymond Hernandez And Stephen Labaton, "In Opposing Tax Plan, Schumer Breaks With Party," *New York Times*, July 30, 2007, http://www.nytimes.com/2007/07/30/washington/30schumer.html?ex=1343448000&en=59c40a9b43932760&ei=5090&partner=rssuserland&emc=rss

35. Eric Lipton and Raymond Hernandez, "A Champion of Wall Street Reaps Benefits," *New York Times*, December 13, 2008, http://www.nytimes.com/2008/12/14/business/14schumer.html?_r=1&hp 36. Ibid.

37. Aviva Aron-Dine, "An Analysis of the 'Carried Interest' Controversy," Center on Budget and Policy Priorities, July 31, 2007, http://www.cbpp.org/7-31-07tax.htm#_ftn5

38. United States Senate Committee on Finance, "The Taxation of Carried Interest," Statement of Peter R. Orszag, Director, Congressional Budget Office, 110th Cong., 1st sess., July 11, 2007, http://www.cbo.gov/doc.cfm?index=8306&type=0

39. Congressman Sandy Levin, "Levin and Democrats Introduce Legislation to End Carried Interest Tax Advantage," press release, June 2, 2007, http://www.house.gov/apps/list/press/mi12_levin/

PR062207.shtml

40. Carried Interest, "Chamber Study Shows Tax Increases on Partnerships Pose A Great Risk to the U.S. Economy," http://www.carriedinterest.org/portal/ci/default

41. Private Equity Council, "About the Private Equity Council," http://www.privateequitycouncil.org/about/

42. Open Secrets, "Private Equity & Investment Firms: Long-Term Contribution Trends," http://www.opensecrets.org/industries/indus.php?ind=F2600

43. Open Secrets, "Hedge Funds: Long-Term Contribution Trends," http://www.opensecrets.org/industries/indus.php?ind=F2700

44. *Reuters*, "Sen. Grassley "still studying" carried interest," November 14, 2007, http://www.reuters.com/article/politicsNews/idUSN1420551320071114

45. William L. Watts, "Senators tackle tax treatment of fund managers," *MarketWatch*, July, 11 2007, http://www.marketwatch.com/News/Story/senator-lashes-back-private-equity-tax/story.aspx?guid={A8EB3189-F2F6-4FBF-A294-2B56D3D9FC2A}

46. Raymond Hernandez and Stephen Labaton, "In Opposing Tax Plan, Schumer Supports Wall Street Over Party," *New York Times*, July 30, 2007.

47. Lindsay Renick Mayer, "Capitol Eye Blog: Obama's Pick for Chief of Staff Tops Recipients of Wall Street Money," Open Secrets, November 5, 2008, http://www.opensecrets.org/news/2008/11/obamas-pick-for-chief-of-staff.html

Conclusion: A Return To Sanity

1. Organizing for America, "Poverty," http://www.barackobama.com/issues/poverty/index_campaign.php

2. To provide for comprehensive health insurance coverage for all United States residents, and for other purposes, HR 676, 108th Cong., 1st sess., http://frwebgate.access.gpo.gov/cgi-bin/getdoc.cgi?dbname=108_cong_bills&docid=f:h676ih.txt.pdf

3. Physicians for a National Health Program, "Single-Payer National

Health Insurance," http://www.pnhp.org/facts/single_payer_re-sources.php

4. Dean Baker, "Universal Voluntary Accounts: A Step Towards Fixing the Retirement System," Center for Economic and Policy Research, December 2006, http://www.cepr.net/index.php/publications/reports/universal-voluntary-accounts-a-step-towards-fixing-the-retirement-system/

5. Ibid.

6. Jose Garcia, "Borrowing to Make Ends Meet: The Rapid Growth of Credit Card Debt in America," Demos, November 7, 2007 http://www.demos.org/pubs/stillborrowing.pdf; Federal Reserve Statistical Release, "Consumer Credit," July 8, 2009, http://www.federalreserve.gov/releases/g19/Current/

7. Ibid.

8. David Madland and Karla Walter, "Unions Are Good for the American Economy," Center for American Progress Action Fund, February 18, 2009, http://www.americanprogressaction.org/issues/2009/02/efca_factsheets.html

9. Ibid.

10. Brian Montopoli, "Primer: The Big Battle Between Business And Unions," CBS News, March 10, 2009 http://www.cbsnews.com/blogs/2009/03/10/politicalhotsheet/entry4856849.shtml

11. Business Week, "Employee Free Choice Act: Labor vs. Business," September 22, 2008.

12. Michael Luo And Christopher Drew, "Big Donors, Too, Have Seats at Obama Fund-Raising Table," New York Times, August 5, 2008, http://www.nytimes.com/2008/08/06/us/politics/06bundlers.html

13. David D. Kirkpatrick, "Death Knell May Be Near for Public Election Funds," New York Times, January 23, 2007, http://www.nytimes.com/2007/01/23/us/politics/23donate.html

14. Common Cause, "Clean Elections for the United States Congress," http://www.commoncause.org/site/pp.asp?c=dkLNK1MQIwG&b=4104607

15. Theodore Roosevelt, "State of the Union," December 3, 1907, http://

www.let.rug.nl/~usa/P/tr26/speeches/tr_1907.htm

16. Carl Hulse and David M. Herszenhorn, "House Approves 90% Tax on Bonuses After Bailouts," *New York Times*, March 19, 2009, http://www.nytimes.com/2009/03/20/business/20bailout.html?scp=1&sq=90%20percent%20AIG&st=Search

17. *Financial Times*, "Banker Fury Over Tax 'Witch-hunt'", March 21, 2009, http://www.ft.com/cms/s/0/71b06878-15b7-11de-b9a9-0000779fd2ac.html?nclick_check=1

18. Brian Knowlton, "McCain Faults Detainee Treatment, and Auto Industry," *New York Times*, December 14, 2008, http://thecaucus.blogs.nytimes.com/2008/12/14/mccain-urges-bankruptcy-like-solution-for-auto-makers/?scp=5&sq=anti-UAW&st=Search

19. David M. Herszenhorn and Bill Vlasic, "Auto Executives Still Find Skeptics," *New York Times*, December 4, 2008, http://www.nytimes.com/2008/12/05/business/05auto.html?pagewanted=1&sq=auto%20executives%20congress&st=Search&scp=2

20. Herman E. Daly, "Economics in a full world," *Scientific American* 293 no. 3 (2005): 100-107.

21. Herman E. Daly, "Boundless Bull," *Gannett Center Journal* 4 no. 3 (Summer 1990):113-118.

22. U.S. Congress, Office of Technology Assessment, *Multinationals and the National Interest: Playing By Different Rules* (Washington, DC: Government Printing Office, September 1993).

23. Redefining Progress, "Genuine Progress Indicator," http://www.rprogress.org/sustainability_indicators/genuine_progress_indicator.htm

24. Joel Rogers has written about this extensively. The above quotation is contained in a July 2005 memo to the author.